COMMENTARY ON FOUR SURAS

Spider عنكبوت

Beneficent رحمن

Event واقعه

Kingdom ملك

THE MERCY OF QUR'ÃN AND THE ADVENT OF ZAMÃN

COMMENTARY ON FOUR SURAS

TAFSÎR BY

SHAYKH FADHLALLA HAERI

ZAHRA PUBLICATIONS
INDIA

Published by :

ZAHRA PUBLICATIONS

R-4, SECTOR 12
NOIDA, U.P. INDIA
PH.: 91-4539954
FAX : 91-4444090
E-mail : mumtaz1@VSNL.Com

Distributed in India by :

Kitab Bhavan

Publishers, Distributors, Exporters & Importers
1784, Kalan Mahal, Darya Ganj
New Delhi-110002 (India)
Phone : (91-11) 3277392/93, 3274686
Web Site : www.kitabbhavan.com
E-mail : nasri@vsnl.com
Fax : (91-11) 3263383

Edition : 2002
ISBN : 81-7151-332-8
Book Code : M00342

CONTENTS

Foreword

The Mercy of Qur'ãn and the Advent of Zamãn is a commentary (*tafsir*) on four selected *suras* of the Holy Qur'ãn, namely: *al-'Ankabut*, *ar-Rahman*, *al-Waqi'a*, and *al-Mulk*. This commentary is part of a series of discourses delivered by Shaykh Fadhlalla Haeri at the American Institute of Qur'anic Studies.

These four Makkan *suras* were chosen because of a strong interconnecting theme. *Al-'Ankabut* is about the affliction of man for the sake of his own upbringing, so he is freed from his illusions and insecure foundations. *Ar-Rahman* demonstrates the direct signs and marks of the Creator wherever one looks. *Al-Waqi'a* reminds one of the next life so that the pursuit of knowledge and submission to the Creator in this life becomes urgent and vital. *Al-Mulk* shows that if there were such things as other deities, they would all ultimately have to be under the one and only God, in Whose hand rests total harmony and control.

The commentary opens up some of the great vistas of the inner meanings of the Qur'ãn. While the reader is guided to the bounties of the Qur'ãnic message through allegorical interpretation of the Qur'ãnic language, he is at once shown the path of safe conduct in this world and the hereafter. The all-pervading message is of balance and mercy. The key to this attainment is self-knowledge. The commentary explicates man's station with reference to his Creator and how the entire creation sings the song of *tawhîd*—divine unity. It compels the reader to reflect the inter-connectedness in all facets of life. These four suras show the way to the knowledge of the one Creator and warn man as to his failure and injustice towards himself by not adhering to the path of love and submission.

(٢٩) سُورَةُ العَنكَبُوتِ مَكِّيَّة
وَآيَاتُهَا تِسْعٌ وَسِتُّونَ

SURAT UL-ANKABUT

THE SPIDER

Introduction

Whoever professes, confesses, or witnesses the one Creator of creation in all its diversity will undergo the strengthening process of affliction. Duality and association with the one Creator will gradually be worn away from him. In Arabic, the verb to afflict also means to become old and worn.

Some of the early Muslims in Makkah could not withstand the pressure exerted upon them to return to the convenience of old habits. This *sura* historically reflects that situation in Makkah. The name of the *sura* refers to the flimsy, insecure home or structure on which we tend to depend, like the spider's web. The only structure which is indestructible is based on the knowledge of God and His laws that govern existence.

بِسْمِ اللَّهِ الرَّحْمَٰنِ الرَّحِيمِ

In the Name of Allah, the Beneficent, the Merciful.

الٓمٓ

1 **Alif Lam Mim.**

اَحَسِبَ النَّاسُ اَنْ يُّتْرَكُوٓا اَنْ يَّقُوْلُوٓا اٰمَنَّا وَ هُمْ لَا يُفْتَنُوْنَ

2 **Do men think that they will be left alone on saying, we believe, and not be tried?**

وَلَقَدْ فَتَنَّا الَّذِينَ مِن قَبْلِهِمْ فَلَيَعْلَمَنَّ اللَّهُ الَّذِينَ
صَدَقُوا وَلَيَعْلَمَنَّ الْكَاذِبِينَ

3 **And certainly We tried those before them, so Allah will certainly know those who are true and He will certainly know the liars.**

There is a purpose in creation, a visible, subtle, and deep purpose, which is to discover the meaning of existence. However, man must trust in Allah in order to fully commit himself to the quest. No matter how hard man may try to reckon and calculate the purpose of this existence, he will not succeed without *îmãn* (ايمان , trust), which has its root in the heart. Deflection from this ultimate source will only result in *fitna* (فتنه), which is trial, affliction and discord.

Fitna implies superficial trial or affliction. It is a plot, that seems charming and captivating; but a plot can be easily discovered—it is not substantial. A *fatin* (فاتن) is a woman who decorates herself to attract a man, hiding what may be a most dreadful character. No matter how man reckons or calculates, he will be afflicted in a superficial way so that his *îmãn*, his trust, becomes more real and certain of the absolute and not of the relative. Trust begins in the outward and existential but leads to the inward. There is no separation of the deep inner reality and the outer reality because they are a continuum. There is no end to Reality. It is only for the sake of illustration that we talk about the outer and the inner.

Fitna is derived from the verb *fatana* (فتن), which amongst other things, means to prove. *Dinar maftun* (دينار مفتون) is a gold coin that has been tested and proven to be true gold. Imam Hasan, *'alayhi-s-salãm* (عليه السلام , upon him be peace), defined *fitna* as that which proves man's reality, his divine origin, by what appears to be affliction, turmoil and trouble. Divine mercy puts man through processes that appear to be undesirable and troublesome, showing man that he has no power over anything. Man has, in fact, no claim over anything except the witnessing and the recognition of the One and Only---*La ilaha illa-llah* (لا اله الا الله).

اَمْ حَسِبَ الَّذِينَ يَعْمَلُونَ السَّيِّاتِ اَنْ يَّسْبِقُونَا سَآءَ
مَا يَحْكُمُونَ

4 **Or do they who work evil think that they will escape Us? Evil is it that they judge!**

مَنْ كَانَ يَرْجُوا لِقَآءَ اللّٰهِ فَاِنَّ اَجَلَ اللّٰهِ لَاٰتٍ ج وَهُوَ
السَّمِيعُ الْعَلِيمُ

5 **Whoever hopes to meet Allah, the term of Allah will then most surely come; and He is the Hearing, the Knowing.**

وَمَنْ جَاهَدَ فَاِنَّمَا يُجَاهِدُ لِنَفْسِهٖ ط اِنَّ اللّٰهَ لَغَنِيٌّ عَنِ
الْعٰلَمِينَ

6 **And whoever strives hard, he strives only for himself; most surely Allah is Self-sufficient, above (need of) the worlds.**

وَالَّذِينَ اٰمَنُوا وَعَمِلُوا الصّٰلِحٰتِ لَنُكَفِّرَنَّ عَنْهُمْ
سَيِّاٰتِهِمْ وَلَنَجْزِ يَنَّهُمْ اَحْسَنَ الَّذِى كَانُوْا يَعْمَلُونَ

7 **And (as for) those who believe and do good, We will most certainly do away with their evil deeds and We will most certainly reward them the best of what they did.**

Man in his arrogance and cleverness thinks that he can escape from the prescribed laws governing existence. He thinks he can cheat Allah and imagines himself as a separate entity, which is *shirk* (شرک , associating other-than-Allah with Allah). The nature of he who has complete and utter trust is that he does not see himself; he sees only one higher Self. He sees himself and his actions only as an outer manifestation of oneness. He has absolute security, certainty, serenity and independence by having discovered dependence on Allah. The opposite of this *tawhîd*(توحيد ,divine unity) is man's imagination that he exists alongside Allah. Full dependence on Allah brings about independence because man becomes independent of other-than-Allah.

Love of Reality guides and draws man towards *tawhîd*. If he claims trust in Reality, that claim will be put to the test. It is Allah's mercy by which He helps man to recognize the degree of his sincerity and honesty. The *îmãn* of the early followers of the Prophet Muhammad, *sallah-llãhu 'alayhi wa ãlihi wa sallam* (صلى الله عليه واله وسلم) was tested; pressure was exerted upon them by the prevailing system which saw this revolutionary message as a threat to its own survival. Many families urged their relatives who followed Muhammad, *sallah-llãhu 'alayhi wa ãlihi wa sallam* (peace and blessings be upon him and his family), to return to the traditional, inherited and ignorant ways. Some had one or both of their parents threaten to take their lives and the lives of their offspring in order to deflect them from diving deeper into their belief.

For those who remain in *îmãn* is the promise that they will come to know Allah and the truth of the Resurrection. The more they exert themselves in this life, the closer they will get to this state of knowledge. The *mu'minun* (مؤمنون ,believers) are given a clear code of conduct. By righteously doing their utmost they will be amply rewarded.

وَوَصَّيْنَا الْإِنْسَانَ بِوَالِدَيْهِ حُسْناً ط وَإِنْ جَاهَدَاكَ
لِتُشْرِكَ بِي مَالَيْسَ لَكَ بِهِ عِلْمٌ فَلَا تُطِعْهُمَا ط إِلَيَّ
مَرْجِعُكُمْ فَأُنَبِّئُكُم بِمَا كُنْتُمْ تَعْمَلُونَ

8 **And We have enjoined on man goodness to his parents, and if they contend with you that you should associate (others) with Me, of which you have no knowledge, do not obey them; to Me is your return, so I will inform you of what you did.**

وَالَّذِينَ آمَنُوا وَعَمِلُوا الصَّالِحَاتِ لَنُدْخِلَنَّهُمْ فِي
الصَّالِحِينَ

9 **And (as for) those who believe and do good, We will most surely cause them to enter among the good.**

The first thing a child witnesses is his parents. If he does not show loyalty towards them, he cannot show loyalty in a subtler way towards Allah. A child's rebellion against his parents is a rebellion against all those who have physical power over him and sustain him. If a child is rebellious against his parents, he is likely to be rebellious against anything. The parents may be, from a spiritual point of view, misguided, but the child can only be qualified to reflect upon or witness that when his own self-guidance begins to emerge. Irrespective of anything, the child should have compassion for them.

Under all circumstances, a person is advised to be respectful to his parents. It does not mean he is to be under their domination, but when their names are mentioned, he should ask for their forgiveness. After all, they were the means by which he had come about Regardless of whether one is good or bad one still has the mercy of the Creator upon him. Allah is the invisible origin from which man has come forth through his parents.

There are various degrees of *îmãn*. A true *mu'min* regards everything that happens to him as his destiny. It must be, for it has occurred and is itself the proof of its truth and reality. It has occurred not out of a whim but from Reality. A *mu'min* takes knowledge from everything, whether it appears to be good or bad. If he has not identified himself with a specific, fixed viewpoint, he will derive knowledge and benefit from affliction.

وَمِنَ النَّاسِ مَنْ يَّقُولُ اٰمَنَّا بِاللّٰهِ فَاِذَآ اُوذِیَ فِی اللّٰهِ جَعَلَ
فِتْنَةَ النَّاسِ كَعَذَابِ اللّٰهِ ط وَلَئِنْ جَآءَ نَصْرٌ مِّنْ رَّبِّكَ لَيَقُولُنَّ
اِنَّا كُنَّا مَعَكُمْ ط اَوَلَيْسَ اللّٰهُ بِاَعْلَمَ بِمَا فِی صُدُورِ الْعٰلَمِينَ

10 **And among men is he who says: We believe in Allah; but when he is persecuted in (the way of) Allah he thinks the persecution of men to be as the chastisement of Allah; and if there come assistance from your lord, they would most certainly say: Surely we were with you. What! is not Allah the best knower of what is in the breasts of mankind.**

وَلَيَعْلَمَنَّ اللّٰهُ الَّذِينَ اٰمَنُوا وَلَيَعْلَمَنَّ الْمُنٰفِقِينَ

11 **And most certainly Allah will know those who believe, and most certainly He will know the hypocrites.**

The aspect most difficult for the *nafs* (نفس, lower self) to witness is hypocrisy. Most actions are justified in a hypocritical way. A man may say he is working *fi sabili-llah* (in the way of Allah), but may actually want to gain a high reputation, or become the *imam* امام) of a community or the leader of a country. If his actions are for Allah's sake the afflictions from people will drive him more towards the source, into his innermost, into dependence upon Reality. The people themselves are not in awareness but they are nonetheless a reflection of Reality to the *mu'mi'n*.

Because that reflection may not be seen clearly, those who are weak in their trust and do not derive wisdom and spiritual growth from events, may read afflictions brought about by the wrongdoings of man as being signs that Allah is punishing them, that Allah is not rewarding them for being on the path of *îmãn*. The weak at heart look for signs in order to weaken themselves further. The man of discrimination simply dismisses such occurrences as men's injustices. It is an imposition, a natural occurrence which strengthens those who are strong at heart, strong in *îmãn*, and weakens those who are weak at heart. It is nature's way of sifting out those without wisdom.

وَقَالَ الَّذِينَ كَفَرُوا لِلَّذِينَ آمَنُوا اتَّبِعُوا سَبِيلَنَا
وَلْنَحْمِلْ خَطَايَاكُمْ ۖ وَمَا هُمْ بِحَامِلِينَ مِنْ خَطَايَاهُمْ
مِنْ شَيْءٍ ۖ إِنَّهُمْ لَكَاذِبُونَ

12 **And those who disbelieve say to those who believe: Follow our path and we will bear your wrongs. And never shall they be the bearers of any of their wrongs; most surely they are liars.**

وَلَيَحْمِلُنَّ أَثْقَالَهُمْ وَأَثْقَالًا مَعَ أَثْقَالِهِمْ ۖ وَلَيُسْأَلُنَّ يَوْمَ
الْقِيَامَةِ عَمَّا كَانُوا يَفْتَرُونَ

13 **And most certainly they shall carry their own burdens, and other burdens with their own burdens, and most certainly they shall be questioned on the resurrection day as to what they forged.**

The early people, when their *îmãn* was weak, when other people were causing them trouble, wanted to give up their belief in the Prophet Muhammad, *sallah-llãhu 'alayhi wa ãlihi wa sallam.* They claimed that Allah was sending them messages in the form of afflictions, indicating that they should take the path of least resistance. But it was the path of expediency that they wanted to follow, and therefore, in time would become the more difficult path. Afflictions are the test of nature upon man. Those who turned away from the right path lacked discrimination and *imam*. They read into the signs the most obvious meanings, without considering the direction in which they were being led.

What occurred at the dawn of Islam is repeated at all times. It is man who reads loss into afflictions. This has nothing to do with Reality. A sign is sent by Allah in order that the *mu'min* recognizes that the others are wrongly guided. Man reads into signs what he wishes according to the strength of his *îmãn* and the purity of his intention. Allah says: "My mercy encompasses everything." Man must try to see it. The law is there, written; it is up to him to penetrate into the subtleties of how that law operates at all times, under all circumstances, everywhere and for everyone. Allah's mercy is instantaneous and the degree of its being seen, felt and tasted is the degree of the sincerity of one's *îmãn*.

وَلَقَدْ اَرْسَلْنَا نُوحًا اِلٰى قَوْمِهٖ فَلَبِثَ فِيهِمْ اَلْفَ سَنَةٍ
اِلَّا خَمْسِينَ عَامًا فَاَخَذَهُمُ الطُّوفَانُ وَهُمْ ظٰلِمُونَ

14 **And certainly We sent Nûh to his people, so he remained among them a thousand years save**

fifty years. And the deluge overtook them, while they were unjust.

فَأَنجَيْنَاهُ وَأَصْحَابَ السَّفِينَةِ وَجَعَلْنَاهَا آيَةً لِّلْعَالَمِينَ

15 **So We delivered him and the inmates of the ark, and made it a sign to the nations.**

The Prophet, *sallah-llãhu 'alayhi wa ãlihi wa sallam,* said: "My example and the example of the close and selected members of my family is like the ship of *Nûh* (Noah): he who rides in it will be safe, but he who does not will flounder."

If man takes on the conduct of the Prophet and his family, carrying a passport issued from their way, he will move safely from one port to another. He will pass from the port of mortality to the port of immortality. If he does not, he will flounder and at best be confused. That is the state of the majority of people whether or not they call themselves Muslims. They do not hold to His rope. The Qur'ãn says very clearly: Those of you that want to follow Allah and know Him, follow the Prophet, follow what he stood for and what he reflected. Follow in the footsteps of those who came after him. A *Hadith* (حديث, tradition, saying) says: "Men of knowledge are the heirs of the prophets." What is there to inherit from a prophet but his knowledge and its application in one's life?

In existence everything we witness is based on duality, such as life and death, guidance and misguidance, leading and being led. Man experiences opposites simultaneously. He loves and hates simultaneously. If a man loves truth, justice, compassion and generosity, then he is bound to hate injustice, tyranny and meanness.

By understanding and actually experiencing this concept man can guide his actions toward the higher opposites so that they emanate from the opposites that are closer to the attributes of Reality. He recognizes that he has travelled a great distance from the lower tendencies toward the higher tendencies. He has left fear and insecurity and approaches positiveness, secure in the knowledge that he will come to know and be able to improve the quality of life around him.

وَإِبْرٰهِيمَ إِذْ قَالَ لِقَوْمِهِ اعْبُدُوا اللّٰهَ وَاتَّقُوهُ ط ذٰلِكُمْ
خَيْرٌ لَّكُمْ إِنْ كُنتُمْ تَعْلَمُونَ

16 **And (We sent) Ibrahim, when he said to his people: Serve Allah and be careful of (your duty to) Him; this is best for you, if you did but know.**

إِنَّمَا تَعْبُدُونَ مِنْ دُونِ اللّٰهِ أَوْثَانًا وَّتَخْلُقُونَ إِفْكًا ط إِنَّ
الَّذِينَ تَعْبُدُونَ مِنْ دُونِ اللّٰهِ لَا يَمْلِكُونَ لَكُمْ رِزْقًا فَابْتَغُوا
عِنْدَ اللّٰهِ الرِّزْقَ وَاعْبُدُوهُ وَاشْكُرُوا لَهُ ط إِلَيْهِ تُرْجَعُونَ

17 **You only worship idols besides Allah and you create a lie; surely they whom you serve besides Allah do not control for you any sustenance, therefore seek the sustenance from Allah and serve Him and be grateful to Him; to Him you shall be brought back.**

وَإِنْ تُكَذِّبُوا فَقَدْ كَذَّبَ أُمَمٌ مِّنْ قَبْلِكُمْ ط وَمَا عَلَى
الرَّسُولِ إِلَّا الْبَلٰغُ الْمُبِينُ

18 **And if you reject (the truth), nations before you did indeed reject (the truth); and nothing is**

incumbent on the apostle but a clear delivering (of the message).

Follow those who possess *ulu' ul- amr* (اولو الامر), those who possess that command by *idhn* (اذن, permission), hold the order in their hands and can interpret it. The order of Allah is the way of Allah, which is the recognition of the truth and reality that comes by abandonment and submission into the one and only Reality. Outer order and command brings about physical order. The order of Allah is in the purpose of His creation which is that His highest creation, man, should come to know His will as it manifests in His laws which govern existence.

Man stumbles on in his life with the purpose of knowing the laws that govern right and wrong action. Affliction and turmoil are only the natural means for man to come to know the boundaries so that he does not transgress them, so that he knows at what point he is beginning to cause himself harm. The *ulu ul- amr* are the people who know the order of affairs, who have wisdom and the innate, innermost knowledge that there is only Reality and that It manifests in every man and form. Taking on their knowledge is bound to lead one to success and not to self-harm.

Man has no control over what he may inherit. It may be that a people must pay back a debt accumulated by those who came earlier. If a man has abused his land, his children will start off with a handicap which they can do nothing about except seek to overcome it over a period of time. That again is the Reality. If they had knowledge, they would recognize their difficult situation and make allowances for it and not be disappointed.

Ulu' ul-amr is often misunderstood. Tyrants throughout the history of Islam, acting selfishly and despotically, simply interpreted it as 'those who are in power'. It is generally recognized that those who are in power do not deserve to be. They do not represent the highest in man.

According to the true followers of the Muhammadi light, as exemplified by the holy *Ahl ul-Bayt* (اهل البيت , the Prophet's family) and illustrated amply by Imam Ja'far as-Sadiq, *'alayhi-s-salãm*, the *ulu' ul- amr* are those who deserve to be leading us to the knowledge of Allah. They have gained authority first and foremost over their lower tendencies and have knowledge that can lead others to ultimate bliss, in this life, by correct conduct, working and living in a manner that befits man, the highest of creation.

People who have often strayed off the true path use *taqiyya* (تقية , dissimulation of one's religion) to excuse themselves from *jihãd* (جهاد , utmost exertion in the cause of righteousness) or from exercising energy and doing their utmost as part of the will of Reality. Everything is evolving towards the higher. Man must also reflect that by doing his utmost to change circumstances that are wrong and cast dark shadows of ignorance.

Life is based upon dynamic movement. It echoes the meaning of *samadiyya,* foreverness. Perpetuity manifests from within us. Often man is fearful of dynamic movement, but he is much better off guarding against downward movement within himself and his conscience. A man of *taqwa* (تقوى , fearful awareness) fears only Allah while showing complete fearlessness in his actions. Yet he is not disrespectful nor does he promote chaos. Everything has its boundary and its *adab* (ادب , courtesy).

أَوَلَمْ يَرَوْا كَيْفَ يُبْدِئُ اللَّهُ الْخَلْقَ ثُمَّ يُعِيدُهُ ۚ إِنَّ ذَٰلِكَ
عَلَى اللَّهِ يَسِيرٌ

19 **Do they not see how Allah originates the creation, then reproduces it? Surely that is easy to Allah.**

Creation follows the cycle of beginning, maturing, ending and then recreating. Recreation is the reflection of creation in the timeless zone. The brief flicker of creation is a hint of the state of being frozen in absolute non-time in the next life.

Man loves the 'beyond time'. He cannot do without sleep which is the nearest he can taste of timelessness in this life. Some people have had the opportunity of a near fatal accident and have experienced a similitude of death. Also, in the state of *dhikr* (ذكر , remembrance), in what the sufis call *fana'* (فناء , self-obliteration), there is a death of meaning. Life is a cycle of creation and recreation. As this creation came and went, so will another creation begin with a resurrection (*ba'th*, بعث) As man rose into wakefulness, so will another form of rising occur in a purer energy form without the physical matter which belongs to this little speck called earth.

قُلْ سِيرُوا فِي الْأَرْضِ فَانظُرُوا كَيْفَ بَدَأَ الْخَلْقَ ثُمَّ اللَّهُ
يُنشِئُ النَّشْأَةَ الْآخِرَةَ ۚ إِنَّ اللَّهَ عَلَىٰ كُلِّ شَيْءٍ قَدِيرٌ

20 **Say: Travel in the earth and see how He makes the first creation, then Allah creates the latter creation; surely Allah has power over all things.**

يُعَذِّبُ مَن يَشَاءُ وَيَرْحَمُ مَن يَشَاءُ ۖ وَإِلَيْهِ تُقْلَبُونَ

21 **He punishes whom He pleases and has mercy on whom He pleases, and to Him you shall be turned back.**

وَمَآ أَنتُم بِمُعْجِزِينَ فِي الْأَرْضِ وَلَا فِي السَّمَآءِ وَمَا
لَكُم مِّن دُونِ اللَّهِ مِن وَلِيٍّ وَلَا نَصِيرٍ

22 **And you shall not escape in the earth nor in the heaven, and you have neither a protector nor a helper besides Allah.**

The nature of existence is that of a journey. Everything is based on movement. The electrons journey around the nucleus and the earth journeys through space. The first thing a newborn child does is to move. The entire creation is a journey from Allah, to Allah, by Allah, and the highest benefit for man comes if he emulates it by journeying into the land.

In every way it is a blessing to travel. In the *Shadhili tariqa* (طريقة , a Sufi path), the masters never slept in one place for more than three weeks, so as not to take what was around them for granted. *Haraka ma'a-l-baraka* (حركة مع بركة): movement is with blessing. Man must change, he must move on so that he does not become a slave of outer habits and become fixated. Man is attracted to fixation because he loves the permanent, the ever-fixed within him. But to desire preservation of outer fixation is ignorance. The outer can never be fixed. No sooner does man try to control an event than he finds it beyond his power to do so.

Man wants to know the permanent but he mistakenly tries to bring it about in his environment by establishing rigid habits. At the lowest, most superficial level, travel disturbs this tendency. The earth would be sterile if it were not disturbed, if it were not plowed. The same thing applies to man's heart. If it is not disturbed, if it is not cut off from its desires and attachments, how can it resonate and keep turning? At first one resents being cut off, but the purpose of one's life is to move both outwardly and inwardly; outwardly by having dynamic attitudes toward the world and the earth, and inwardly by being willing to turn away from what the self desires.

Travel *fi sabili-llah* is a very blessed outer activity. A *sa'ih* (سائح) at one time meant a man traveling for Allah, calling people to the *din* (دين , life-transaction). He was a *mubashshir*, (مبشّر, deliverer of good tidings) following the way of those who give the bushr (بشر , the good news). Now *siyaha*, (سياحة) which used to mean travelling *fi sabili-llah*, means tourism. Tourism today is synonymous with irresponsibility, as it enhances outer greed and appetite, whereas previously travelling from one culture to another promoted inner growth and fulfillment.

وَالَّذِينَ كَفَرُوا بِآيَاتِ اللَّهِ وَلِقَائِهِ أُولَٰئِكَ يَئِسُوا مِن رَّحْمَتِي وَأُولَٰئِكَ لَهُمْ عَذَابٌ أَلِيمٌ

23 **And (as to) those who disbelieve in the communications of Allah and His meeting, they have despaired of My mercy, and these it is that shall have a painful punishment.**

فَمَا كَانَ جَوَابَ قَوْمِهِ إِلَّا أَن قَالُوا اقْتُلُوهُ أَوْ حَرِّقُوهُ فَأَنجَاهُ اللَّهُ مِنَ النَّارِ ۚ إِنَّ فِي ذَٰلِكَ لَآيَاتٍ لِّقَوْمٍ يُؤْمِنُونَ

24 **So naught was the answer of his people except that they said: Slay him or burn him! Then Allah delivered him from the fire;most surely there are signs in this for a people who believe.**

وَقَالَ إِنَّمَا اتَّخَذْتُم مِّن دُونِ اللَّهِ أَوْثَانًا مَّوَدَّةَ بَيْنِكُمْ فِي الْحَيَاةِ الدُّنْيَا ۖ ثُمَّ يَوْمَ الْقِيَامَةِ يَكْفُرُ بَعْضُكُم بِبَعْضٍ وَيَلْعَنُ بَعْضُكُم بَعْضًا وَمَأْوَاكُمُ النَّارُ وَمَا لَكُم مِّن نَّاصِرِينَ

25 **And he said: You have only taken for yourselves idols besides Allah by way of friendship between you in this world's life, then on the resurrection day some of you shall deny others, and some of you will curse others, and your abode is the fire, and you will not have any helpers.**

The creation of Allah, having come from Allah, must already intrinsically know Allah and therefore already have met Allah. But He is forgotten by man, hidden by the visible and solid. The *shari'a* (شريعة , outward path) of existence overwhelms the *haqiqa* (حقيقة , inner truth). The *shahada* (شهادة , testimonial witnessing) is said aloud in the belief that its reality will bewitnessed. Everything one sees is from Allah. If it can be named, its essence is derived from the mercy of the *Latif* (اللطيف , the Subtle, the Kind); its *kathif* (كثف, thickness) is derived from subtlety.

The seeker is the one who follows the path of abandonment and submission. Giving in unquestioningly, he finds that there is no question and only Allah. He gets to the root of his affairs. His transactions in life become correct, provided there is the recognition that all has emanated from one merciful Source. He is then on a straight path, acting and not reacting. He is not reacting to something that is within himself, such as insecurity. Yet even insecurity is Allah's love, forcing man to seek the ultimate security. It is the love of Allah that he finds when he moves from one object of security to another. He thinks it is in the wife, mother, father, children or money, but it is in none of them. This is the true *shahada*.

Awakening starts with rejection of what is not: there is no God—*la ilaha* (لا اله). When the seeker, the witnesser, has excluded all, he says: but Allah --- *illa-llah* (الا الله). After negation comes confirmation. It is "The path of those upon whom You have bestowed favors. Not (the path) of those upon whom Your wrath is brought down, nor of those who go astray." (*al-Fatiha*:7)

Al-Liqa' (اللقاء , the meeting) is with Allah, as promised by Him, as will be witnessed by all in the next phase of life, after death. The resurrection, *ba'th*, is the meaning of the meeting. Everyone will then know that there was only Reality acting throughout his previous life. That knowledge will be untarnished or uncolored by emotional connotation or attachment. If knowledge of Allah is attained before death then the being, the soul, will embark onto the next life in that state. If it is not, and the soul is still entrapped by what it has spun in its previous life, then the being will be afflicted in the eternal fire.

"So naught was the answer of his people except that they said: Slay him or burn him!" Ibrahim, *'alayhi-s-salãm*, was put through the fire in this life. Because he had knocked down their idols, his people came to him in anger, asking for an explanation. He said: If they are gods, ask the big one which I have spared to remake the small ones which I have broken. Furious, they made a fire and threw him in. Ibrahim, *'alayhi-s-salãm*, knew that the key to the garden was within himself. He already knew the meaning of the fire in its absolute form. He had saved himself from his inner fire so he was not afraid of the outer fire. Similarly it has been documented in our time that in the state of complete fearlessness, people have been seen to walk great distances on hot coals. This is true *îmãn*.

Man is given a long life in order to seek its purpose; and every time he questions he falls into a hole. This life is Allah's *madrasa* (مدرسة , school) within which man is constantly enrolled, in order to grow and learn. If he can reflect on his life he will find unending lessons.

What we may consider as supernatural, such as walking in fire, is natural. It is exceptional but it does occur. Because man is so distracted, he considers those events to be unnatural. How often do events unfold in which someone is miraculously saved? A man is saved every second by the fact that he is given air by breathing in and out. He is hanging on air but he does not remember. He takes it for granted because he is gross.

"And he said: You have only taken idols besides Allah..." People who have denied themselves access to the path of mercy, who have denied themselves movement or direction towards that which man has been created for in this life, will be in denial in the next life. If he denies now, he will in time be cut off and disconnected. Whenever one does not see the mercy of Allah in a situation, he has fallen. It is a taste of the fire, of anger or disturbance. It is a taste of something that never takes root. The fire is constant agitation and it does not allow anything to hold fast or grow.

But everyone has tasted bliss and momentary contentment. Those who want to have joy in this life will have access to it. They will be in their *nafs*-workshop, cutting and filing the key to joy. The cause of one's trouble is expectation and attachment: this is the key to the door of hell. Since life is dynamic, you are preparing either one of the two keys. You either progress or regress, deriving spiritual nourishment or deficiency.

فَآمَنَ لَهُ لُوطٌ ۘ وَقَالَ إِنِّي مُهَاجِرٌ إِلَىٰ رَبِّي ۖ إِنَّهُ
هُوَ الْعَزِيزُ الْحَكِيمُ

26 **And Lut believed in Him, and he said: I am an emigrant to my Lord. Surely He is the Mighty, the Wise.**

وَوَهَبْنَا لَهٗٓ اِسْحٰقَ وَيَعْقُوْبَ وَجَعَلْنَا فِيْ ذُرِّيَّتِهِ النُّبُوَّةَ
وَالْكِتٰبَ وَاٰتَيْنٰهُ اَجْرَهٗ فِي الدُّنْيَا ۚ وَاِنَّهٗ فِي الْاٰخِرَةِ
لَمِنَ الصّٰلِحِيْنَ

27 **And We granted him Ishãq and Ya'qûb, and caused the prophethood and the book to remain in his seed, and We gave him his reward in this world, and in the hereafter he will most surely be among the good.**

وَلُوْطًا اِذْ قَالَ لِقَوْمِهٖٓ اِنَّكُمْ لَتَاْتُوْنَ الْفَاحِشَةَ
مَا سَبَقَكُمْ بِهَا مِنْ اَحَدٍ مِّنَ الْعٰلَمِيْنَ

28 **And (We sent) Lût when he said to his people: Most surely you are guilty of an indecency which none of the nations has ever done before you.**

اَئِنَّكُمْ لَتَاْتُوْنَ الرِّجَالَ وَتَقْطَعُوْنَ السَّبِيْلَ ۙ وَتَاْتُوْنَ فِيْ
نَادِيْكُمُ الْمُنْكَرَ ۭ فَمَا كَانَ جَوَابَ قَوْمِهٖٓ اِلَّآ اَنْ قَالُوا
ائْتِنَا بِعَذَابِ اللّٰهِ اِنْ كُنْتَ مِنَ الصّٰدِقِيْنَ

29 **What! do you come to the males and commit robbery on the highway, and you commit evil deeds in your assemblies? But nothing was the answer of his people except that they said: Bring on us Allah's punishment, if you are one of the truthful.**

قَالَ رَبِّ انْصُرْنِى عَلَى الْقَوْمِ الْمُفْسِدِيْنَ

30 **He said: My Lord! help me against the mischievous people.**

The Prophet Lût, Ibrahim's maternal cousin, *'alayhi-s-salãm*, did his best for his community. His people had transgressed in their actions and were ultimately cut off from the way of nature, of procreation, by their homosexuality. This community was finished. He had tried his best among them, failed and could move no further. There is a limit to what man can do.

Lût, *'alayhi-s-salãm*, said: "I am an emigrant to my Lord." His Lord is everywhere. His Lord is the Lord of destruction, the Lord of creation, the Lord of all. The Prophets and their followers and seekers have to emigrate from what they are used to, to what is better—from good to better, from old habits to freer ones. *Hijra* (هجرة , emigration) is, in meaning and form, the heritage of seekers of truth. A *hadith* from the Prophet, *sallah-llãhu 'alayhi wa ãlihi wa sallam*, relates that if someone has emigrated *fi sabili-llah,* even if it is only a foot, he is already in the garden.

After doing his best amongst a people and finding that the stream is moving against him, a man should not stay, for the society may collapse upon him. Once a situation has fossilized no one can be helped. No healing is possible and the only thing left to do is to jump out. Allah says: Do as Ibrahim did — make *hijra*. All the great Prophets followed his example.

If the *hijra* is truly *fi sabili-llah*, then the *muhajir* (مهاجر emigrant) will be in such a state that Allah will unveil for him His mercy, making his emigration easy. Allah bestowed upon Ibrahim, *'alayhi-s-salãm*, the pure gift of *Ishãq*, and from *Ishãq*, Ya'qûb, *'alayhum-us-salãm*, Both Ibrahim and the mother of

Ishãq were old, she having previously been barren. *Isma'îl, 'alayhi-s-salãm*, is not mentioned here because he is from a wife of Ibrahim who was not barren. *Ishaq* and *Ya'qub* were gifts given to the Prophet Ibrahim, *'alayhi-s-salãm*, when he began his emigration *fi sabili-llah*, and a provision for future generations.

The Prophet Muhammad, *sallah-llãhu 'alayhi wa ãlihi wa sallam*, had many newcomers to Islam whose *îmãn* was not strong; they feared for lack of provisions. They were accustomed to a narrow way of survival, living on the edge of life. The miraculous expansion of Ibrahim's family, *'alayhi-s-salãm*, when his *hijra* began, is a demonstration to Muhammad's followers that if one calls upon the powers of Reality by treading the prophetic path, one will receive openings.

On a journey, the intelligent man will leave behind excess baggage, values that are inadequate. The life one leaves behind could only get one deeper and deeper into trouble. In this way *hijra* is both inward and outward. Inwardly, a man recognizes and avoids what he knows will cause him trouble. Outwardly, he leaves any situation that is not beneficial to him, until he has enough knowledge to re-enter it without harm coming to him. By then his tree of knowledge has put down such roots that the winds that shake it can only make it drop its dead leaves.

Something that may be useful now may not be right in ten months' time. Movement and struggle must be based on spiritual capacity. At first man should go where he is most familiar. He would be completely devastated if he were to travel in south India, having before that never left Chicago. First one travels to Europe and then onward to the jungle, changing the level of struggle slowly, naturally, a step at a time. It is a dynamic process, cybernetic and self-feeding. Biologically man is continuously moving on and growing. If he does not grow inwardly, he will end up having a white beard and the mentality of a small child.

Man brings difficulties upon himself by his own actions. There is no separation between one's outside and inside. The outer gloom or collapse is a reflection of an inner collapse. A derelict house reflects the inward state of its dweller. The pulsating heart of the man or family that inhabits the house has become static, so the house collapses. It is an outer symptom of an inner collapse. If one is not inwardly willing to uphold what is appropriate for human values, it will show outwardly. One can only prop up the outer facade to a limited degree.

وَلَمَّا جَآئَتْ رُسُلُنَآ اِبْرٰهِيْمَ بِالْبُشْرٰى لا قَالُوْآ اِنَّا مُهْلِكُوْآ اَهْلِ هٰذِهِ الْقَرْيَةِ ج اِنَّ اَهْلَهَا كَانُوْا ظٰلِمِيْنَ

31 **And when Our messengers came to Ibrãhîm with the good news, they said: Surely we are going to destroy the people of this town, for its people are unjust.**

قَالَ اِنَّ فِيْهَا لُوْطاً ط قَالُوْا نَحْنُ اَعْلَمُ بِمَنْ فِيْهَا لَنُنَجِّيَنَّهٗ وَاَهْلَهٗٓ اِلَّا امْرَاَتَهٗ ق كَانَتْ مِنَ الْغٰبِرِيْنَ

32 **He said: Surely in it is Lût. They said: We know well who is in it. We shall certainly deliver him and his followers, except his wife; she shall be of those who remain behind.**

The Prophet Ibrãhîm, *'alayhi-s-salãm*, demonstrates the highest use of *'aql* (عقل intellect) and *tawakkul* (توكّل, trust)—combining *haqiqa* with *shari'a*. He is visited by angels and recognizes their mission and their station. He knows that the people of Lût are to be destroyed and in his concern for *Lût, 'alayhi-s-salãm*, he sends a message to him. Ibrahim's trust in Allah assured him that Lût, *'alayhi-s-salãm*, was blessed and that no harm would come to him. But his love and concern for this being in the next town took an outer expression. However great a man of *tawhîd* may be, his human love is bound to express itself so that others may receive the solace of his humanity. His concern is to connect himself with other beings because he is a man living in unity with Reality.

There are many examples in which the Prophet Muhammad, *sallah-llãhu 'alayhi wa ãlihi wa sallam*, behaved in a particular way only for the sake of other people. It was real behavior, not acting, but it was not a reflection of his inward state. It was purely an outward expression for those around him. If one is in *tawhîd*, it is not for oneself but for others that one acts. The man of *tawhîd* simultaneously shows concern and yet is completely certain that all will be well. Those who know his inward state well, know that he is in absolute certainty. Those who do not, still benefit from his concern and charity. It is *tawhîd*, it is not duality.

The worshipper's love for Allah assumes an outer expression in prayers by the formality of bending. His love for his wife takes a formal outer expression in a gift or kindness. There cannot be an inner without an outer. There can be no *haqiqa* without a *shari'a*. You tether your camel then place your trust upon Allah. One cannot trust in Allah by sitting like a lump of dirt. Allah has given man life, a tongue and limbs in order to act—to act for Allah and by Allah.

As a non-separate entity from the one and only Reality man has to exercise his part in the all-encompassing, ecologically connected situation. This is the meaning of 'shaking the palm tree.' Man has to shake the tree of mercy. In a *Hadith* it says that the supplication of those who call out for provision, yet remain in their homes, will not be heard. Man is a part of the total Oneness. If he intends something, he has to lend himself to be the instrument of its execution. He cannot be in separation from it if he expects well-being to come to him; it will operate consistently through him, in him, above him, below him and beside him.

وَلَمَّآ اَنْ جَآءَتْ رُسُلُنَا لُوطًا سِیٓءَ بِهِمْ وَضَاقَ بِهِمْ
ذَرْعًا وَّقَالُوا لَا تَخَفْ وَلَا تَحْزَنْ اِنَّا مُنَجُّوكَ
وَاَهْلَكَ اِلَّا امْرَاَتَكَ كَانَتْ مِنَ الْغٰبِرِينَ

33 **And when Our messengers came to Lût he was grieved on account of them, and he felt powerless (to protect) them. And they said: Fear not, nor grieve; surely we will deliver you and your followers, except your wife; she shall be of those who remain behind.**

اِنَّا مُنْزِلُونَ عَلٰٓى اَهْلِ هٰذِهِ الْقَرْيَةِ رِجْزًا مِّنَ السَّمَآءِ
بِمَا كَانُوا يَفْسُقُونَ

34 **Surely We will cause to come down upon the people of this town a punishment from heaven, because they transgressed.**

وَلَقَدْ تَّرَكْنَا مِنْهَآ اٰيَةًۢ بَيِّنَةً لِّقَوْمٍ يَّعْقِلُونَ

35 **And certainly We have left a clear sign of it for a people who understand.**

The pure messengers, the angels, complete their mission by visiting the Prophet Lût, *'alayhi-s-salãm*. He is concerned with their safety, for they are surrounded by the disgraceful nation of Sodom. They reassure him that they are safe and inform him of the imminent natural affliction that is going to befall the people who have transgressed nature's way. The sign of that destruction can be visibly seen today. The city of Sodom is one of the major archeological sites in the south-eastern part of the Dead Sea.

وَإِلَى مَدْيَنَ أَخَاهُمْ شُعَيْبًا ۙ فَقَالَ يَٰقَوْمِ ٱعْبُدُوا۟ ٱللَّهَ
وَٱرْجُوا۟ ٱلْيَوْمَ ٱلْءَاخِرَ وَلَا تَعْثَوْا۟ فِى ٱلْأَرْضِ مُفْسِدِينَ

36 **And to Madyan (We sent) their brother Shu'aib, so he said: O my people! serve Allah and fear the latter day and do not act corruptly in the land, making mischief.**

فَكَذَّبُوهُ فَأَخَذَتْهُمُ ٱلرَّجْفَةُ فَأَصْبَحُوا۟ فِى دَارِهِمْ جَٰثِمِينَ

37 **But they rejected him, so a severe earthquake overtook them, and they became motionless bodies in their abode.**

وَعَادًا وَثَمُودَا۟ وَقَد تَّبَيَّنَ لَكُم مِّن مَّسَٰكِنِهِمْ ۖ وقف
وَزَيَّنَ لَهُمُ ٱلشَّيْطَٰنُ أَعْمَٰلَهُمْ فَصَدَّهُمْ عَنِ ٱلسَّبِيلِ
وَكَانُوا۟ مُسْتَبْصِرِينَ

38 **And (We destroyed) 'Âd and Thamûd, and from their dwellings (this) is apparent to you indeed; and the Shaitan made their deeds fair-seeming to them, so he kept them back from the path, though they were endowed with intelligence.**

وَقَارُونَ وَفِرْعَوْنَ وَهَامَٰنَ ۖ وَلَقَدْ جَآءَهُم مُّوسَىٰ
بِالْبَيِّنَٰتِ فَاسْتَكْبَرُوا فِى الْأَرْضِ وَمَا كَانُوا سَٰبِقِينَ

39 **And (We destroyed) Qãrûn and Fir'aun and Hãmãn. And certainly Musa came to them with clear arguments, but they behaved haughtily in the land; yet they could not outstrip (Us).**

Lût, *'alayhi-s-salãm*, migrates physically and the destruction occurs. Again in these ãyãt (آيات) people are warned, remain heedless, are afflicted, annihilated and destroyed. It is a warning for this life and the next. Destruction occurs in this life because in Allah's love and mercy for His creation He wants everyone to be made fit for the garden. And that can only happen if it begins now.

Other prophets have gone through the same experiences with different intensities, locations and forms of affliction. The recurring pattern is that of a man of knowledge warning his people, trying to deflect them from misguidance. His success lies in unconcernedly performing his duty towards himself and his Creator. The ultimate reward is his contentment with himself and the fulfillment of his duty towards his conscience. If there is an outward fruition of his efforts, he is grateful. If he does not see it in his lifetime, still he is grateful. His gratitude comes from the fact that he is in this existence and is following the prescribed path that is ingrained in his heart.

There are not two laws but one law that governs all. There are two states, the state of wakefulness here, which is relative, and the state of eternal wakefulness in the next world, which is absolute. The laws of Allah do not change for anyone. The Qur'ãn says that you never find the laws of Allah changing. The essence and the laws that emanate from Him are absolute and unchanging. If man does not want to be subject to change then he dives into the essence.

The laws of gravity do not change for a prophet. The laws of mechanics did not change for Muhammad, *sallah-llãhu 'alayhi wa ãlihi wa sallam*. At '*Uhûd* the arrows flew and broke his teeth. The Prophet, *sallah-llãhu 'alayhi wa ãlihi wa sallam*, saw the laws which his people did not obey; it was, in a sense, for their sake that he outwardly acknowledged his affliction, so as to make them rally around him and follow his knowledge; but the laws did not change for this great and highly tuned being. The laws continued as did his slavehood, which inspired his followers to travel the path of correct behavior.

Man cannot claim to be above the natural laws for they operate at all levels. He cannot overcome the laws that govern life, especially regarding reaction. Action and reaction are equal and opposite. If he commits an act it has its effect and its effect is its reaction, which is as good as the intention behind the action.

فَكُلًّا أَخَذْنَا بِذَنْبِهِ فَمِنْهُم مَّنْ أَرْسَلْنَا عَلَيْهِ حَاصِبًا ج
وَمِنْهُم مَّنْ أَخَذَتْهُ الصَّيْحَةُ وَمِنْهُم مَّنْ خَسَفْنَا بِهِ
الْأَرْضَ وَمِنْهُم مَّنْ أَغْرَقْنَا ج وَمَا كَانَ اللَّهُ لِيَظْلِمَهُمْ
وَلَٰكِن كَانُوا أَنفُسَهُمْ يَظْلِمُونَ

40 So each We punished for his sin; of them was he on whom We sent down a violent storm, and of them was he whom the rumbling overtook, and of them was he whom We made to be swallowed up by the earth, and of them was he whom We drowned. And Allah did not wrong them, but they wronged themselves.

"So each We punished for his sin." Nature obliterates civilizations once the culture and path of correct moral conduct degenerates and decays. Some peoples were drowned, others were swallowed up by great earthquakes or floods, and still more had the affliction of disease and pestilence.

مَثَلُ الَّذِيْنَ اتَّخَذُوْا مِنْ دُوْنِ اللّٰهِ اَوْلِيَآءَ كَمَثَلِ الْعَنْكَبُوْتِ اِتَّخَذَتْ بَيْتًا ؕ وَاِنَّ اَوْهَنَ الْبُيُوْتِ لَبَيْتُ الْعَنْكَبُوْتِ ۘ لَوْ كَانُوْا يَعْلَمُوْنَ

41 **The parable of those who take guardians besides Allah is as the parable of the spider that makes for itself a house; and most surely the frailest of the houses is the spider's house—did they but know.**

اِنَّ اللّٰهَ يَعْلَمُ مَا يَدْعُوْنَ مِنْ دُوْنِهٖ مِنْ شَىْءٍ ؕ وَهُوَ الْعَزِيْزُ الْحَكِيْمُ

42 **Surely Allah knows whatever thing they call upon besides Him; and He is the Mighty, the Wise.**

The spiderweb is totally exposed to the elements of heat, cold, wind and rain. In fact, the web does not protect the spider from anything. Its main function is to provide for the animal its biological continuance by capturing other insects for food. It is the least secure and the least stable of mechanisms. Any human being who believes he is secure, in what he has inherited in terms of cultural habits which are not in line with the divine decree, is then dwelling on as flimsy a premise as that of a spider's web.

One's attachments, phobias and habits are as brittle as the thought that repeatedly brings them about. The ultimate refuge is with Allah. And man takes refuge in Allah if he pursues the knowledge of Reality by realizing that everything other than Allah is relative and unsatisfactory—like the house of the spider; when the rain comes, the web becomes heavy and breaks apart.

Taking refuge in Allah, man leaves what is relative and insecure and orients himself towards what he knows to be the source of everything. He makes himself a refugee from ignorance to knowledge of Allah. The closer he gets to that knowledge, the more he discovers the relativity of everything. Discrimination and wisdom enable him to handle the laws that govern existence more correctly. He finds them simple to deal with and therefore has the least trouble in this existence.

The easiest way to become familiar with the laws of existence is to try to step out of what one is emotionally enmeshed with in one's spiderweb. The web is what a person may weave and consider to be of importance to his heart. If he leaves all of that then his heart has no connection to the illusions. The heart's function is then natural; it is *fitri* (فطرى, innate). Someone who finds he has become too attached to a place or situation, will feel as though his heart has been stripped from him when it is taken away. This is only his imagination.

The spider leaves the torn web behind and spins another one with little trouble. Man will sit and weep and claim bad luck. He has, how ever been given the additional faculty of consciousness. With it he can become aware of being afflicted. He can be conscious of being conscious. If he delves into pure consciousness he can then dwell with the pure Source.

From traditions we know that one hour's reflection is better than the worship of seventy years. Reflecting upon creation is one of the highest actions one can perform in this existence.

Prayer; fasting, and all the pillars of the life transaction are necessarily helpful in the same way as the structure and foundation of a house are helpful to its occupant. Living in the house joyfully is the ultimate purpose and is attained by deep reflection. The best time for one to reflect is when one has been jolted, when one's spiderweb has been torn by the affliction of leaning for support upon something that has disappeared.

Observing the lives of the Prophets, Imams and the *awliya'* (اولياء ,friends of Allah), one finds they were much afflicted. But in their states they recognized their nearness to Allah. It was for them a great blessing and joy. The Prophet, *sallah-llãhu 'alayhi wa ãlihi wa sallam*, on his death bed had only a handful of people around him. The majority of his friends and companions were involved in the arguments and discussions of succession. His affliction was truly great. For people of *haqiqa*, for people who want to see the inside of things, his inward state is what was important. Was he dependent upon the flimsy network of the so-called *sahaba* (صحابة , companions) or was he dependent upon the Creator of the network?

وَتِلْكَ الْاَمْثَالُ نَضْرِبُهَا لِلنَّاسِ ج وَمَا يَعْقِلُهَآ
اِلَّا الْعٰلِمُوْنَ

43 **And (as for) these parables, We set them forth for men, and none understand them but the learned.**

The further one moves along the path, the greater are the afflictions that come from the outside. It is the *sunna* (سنّة ,way) of Allah. The purpose of afflictions is to make man dependent only on Allah and to thereby increase his knowledge. In a sense, Allah is the most jealous. He does not want man, even occasionally, to think that he is benefitting or depending upon anybody else. Yet the courtesy is to thank one who is the vehicle of help, knowing that at any moment he may become his enemy. This is the state of the *'arif* (عارف , one who knows Allah). This is the true inner meaning of one's *din*. All the outer practices are a preparation for inner sight. When the inner sight is correctly set, the outer practices become the reflection of correctness. If the inner is right then the outer is right. If the outer is right then the inner is right.

"And these parables...none understand them but the learned." They seek to see Allah behind everything. Whenever something manifests they want to know its root, they want to see its cause and not to be taken by its effect. For example, if a dear friend turns out to be your enemy, can you be immediately grateful or not? Think of how merciful Allah is that He has caused you to discover this new enemy now, rather than ten years from now. But if you have considered the friendship as a house of *'ankabut* (عنكبوت , spider), as an abode of safety, then the discovery tears you. As a positive human being you admit your error, otherwise the *'ankabut* is better than you, because it goes on without looking back and builds another place of safety while you continue to establish friendships with wounds and negative memories.

The laws of Reality are to be lived by and made into a life pattern, not simply to be talked or written about. Submission is only meaningful for the people of submission, not for those who talk about it. Islam is for those who are in the *dār* (دار , house) of Islam, not for those who study it. If he allows himself—if he is *'alīm* (عليم, knowing, wise), if he is acquiring knowledge, man can fit into the pattern of submission because its essence is within him.

خَلَقَ اللّٰهُ السَّمٰوٰتِ وَالْاَرْضَ بِالْحَقِّ ؕ اِنَّ فِىْ ذٰلِكَ
لَاٰيَةً لِّلْمُؤْمِنِيْنَ

44 **Allah created the heavens and the earth with truth; most surely there is a sign in this for the believers.**

"Allah created the heavens and the earth with truth." There is a sign in every creational entity. Every breath is a stepping stone along the path of knowledge. Everywhere one looks there is a sign from which to learn.

اُتْلُ مَآ اُوْحِىَ اِلَيْكَ مِنَ الْكِتٰبِ وَاَقِمِ الصَّلٰوةَ ؕ اِنَّ الصَّلٰوةَ تَنْهٰى عَنِ الْفَحْشَآءِ وَالْمُنْكَرِ ؕ وَلَذِكْرُ اللّٰهِ اَكْبَرُ ؕ وَاللّٰهُ يَعْلَمُ مَا تَصْنَعُوْنَ

45 **Recite that which has been revealed to you of the Book and keep up prayer; surely prayer keeps (one) away from indecency and evil, and certainly the remembrance of Allah is the greatest, and Allah knows what you do.**

"Recite (read) that which has been revealed to you of the Book." The command applies to all who follow in the Prophet's footsteps; take what comes to you of knowledge and apply it so that it becomes internalized, then move towards Allah. If one tries to take more than one step at a time one is likely to fall. Missing a step on the path is always a weakness. The seeker should move with what is in front of him in the belief that it is the best for him. Then he will benefit from the step or the state and his movement will be as fast as his sureness and absorption. Prayers are a proof and an acknowledgement of glorification and gratitude to this magnificent gift from the Creator.

"And certainly the remembrance of Allah is the greatest." Whatever state man is in, he punctuates it with *Allahu akbar* (God is most great). He may be in absolute exultation of Reality when he is in *ruku'* (ركوع , bowing in prostration) saying, *subhana rabbi-l-'azimi wa bihamdih* (سبحان ربّى العظيم وبحمده), seeing beyond his frailty and forgetfulness the magnificence of the Creator through His creation; but when he stands up he says, *Allahu akbar* (الله اكبر).

There is always *Allahu akbar*. No matter what openings man has, *Allahu akbar*. Allah is greater than what you imagine. No matter what knowledges come to man, *Allahu akbar*, because it is still only within Allah's ocean of knowledge. Allah's remembrance of man is greater than man's remembrance of Him and Allah's remembrance of the believer is greater than the believer's remembrance of Allah—*Allahu akbar*.

وَلَا تُجَادِلُوا اَهْلَ الْكِتٰبِ اِلَّا بِالَّتِى هِىَ اَحْسَنُ اِلَّا
الَّذِيْنَ ظَلَمُوْا مِنْهُمْ وَقُوْلُوْا اٰمَنَّا بِالَّذِىْ اُنْزِلَ اِلَيْنَا وَاُنْزِلَ
اِلَيْكُمْ وَاِلٰهُنَا وَاِلٰهُكُمْ وَاحِدٌ وَّنَحْنُ لَهٗ مُسْلِمُوْنَ

46 **And do not dispute with the followers of the Book except by what is best, except those of them who act unjustly. And say: We believe in that which has been revealed to us and revealed to you, and our God and your God is One, and to Him do we submit.**

This is enjoined upon the Muslims not to argue or discuss with the people who have had a book revealed to them, such as the Christians or the Jews. The Prophet, *sallah-llãhu 'alayhi wa ãlihi wa sallam*, recommended that his followers neither confirm nor deny what they say because his message, the Qur'ãn, would eventually become evident and supercede the knowledge of the Christians and Jews.

An example of this is the simple case of the stoning of the adulterer which was enjoined by the Prophet Ibrãhîm, '*alayhi-s-salãm*, and recon firmed by the Prophet Mûsa, '*alayhi-s-salãm*, and then by the Prophet 'Îsa, '*alayhi-s-salãm*. But in the traditions of questionable authenticity that have been handed down to the Christians, the Prophet 'Isa, '*alayhi-s-salãm*, dismissed the adulteress who was brought to him by witnesses.

He asked them: Which one of you is righteous and has no sin? When none of them could answer, he dismissed the woman. 'Îsa's criterion for freeing the woman was not complete.

The Prophet, *sallah-llãhu 'alayhi wa ãlihi wa sallam*, clearly established the law that there is a need for four sinless, righteous men to have actually observed the act. Recognizing the law transmitted by Muhammad, *sallah-llãhu 'alayhi wa ãlihi wa sallam*, as the perfect law, there is no question of discussion or argument. The Muslim follows what he regards to be the ultimate and perfect law. All that he can do is to say that his Lord and their Lord are one. Diving into the ocean of *tawhîd*, he hopes that they will recognize the perfection of the path of submission.

A book is not necessarily contained within pages. Muslims and seekers must not judge against other paths which do not have one visible book or one visible prophet. A book means a way of conduct. From this point of view the Buddhists may be considered people of the book, (*ahl al-kitab*, اهل الكتاب). A book reveals the nature of Reality and indicates the way towards understanding it. Many cultures of the world have a book, such as the people of China and India. The Christians and Jews are mentioned in the Qur'ãn while the Buddhists and Taoists are not, because the former were there at the time and in the region in which the Qur'ãn was revealed.

The correct behavior towards the people who believe or have had a message from a Prophet is that one should discuss things with them in the best possible way. There are no differences in what the Prophet Muhammad, *sallah-llãhu 'alayhi wa ãlihi wa sallam,* brought and what the other Prophets brought before him. The message is one but it may be distorted or ignored.

The Qur'ãn says to tell the people who follow other religions, other books, that all the paths are but one path. There has been only one path and that is the path of Islam, which is unquestioning submission. By questioning, one cannot get to the source of the question; one remains at the level of hearing the question and decoding its outer manifestation.

وَكَذٰلِكَ اَنْزَلْنَآ اِلَيْكَ الْكِتٰبَ ط فَالَّذِيْنَ اٰتَيْنٰهُمُ الْكِتٰبَ
يُؤْمِنُوْنَ بِهٖ ج وَمِنْ هٰٓؤُلَآءِ مَنْ يُّؤْمِنُ بِهٖ ط وَمَا يَجْحَدُ
بِاٰيٰتِنَآ اِلَّا الْكٰفِرُوْنَ

47 **And thus have We revealed the Book to you. So those whom We have given the Book believe in it, and of these there are those who believe in it, and none deny Our communications except the unbelievers.**

The first stage of getting the book is physically receiving the message through the ears. Today getting the book is taking out something called a book from a library, getting an outer appearance, an outward message. Man will not get it unless its seed or essence is within him. He will acknowledge an outer experience only if he has the faculty and the ability to comprehend it inwardly. If the ability is not there, no matter what sound is made outside, it will not make an impact on him. If the essence is not within his conscious faculties, the Book or any book for that matter, will not make sense to him. He must unify with the message.

Those who have been given the book are those who have received the message and understood it. They have unified the outward message or teaching with their inner reflection and awakening. Their belief cannot be taken away from them. An outer sound has connected to an inner resonance. An outer message has connected with an inner call that had been dormant. The outer message activated the inner light and made it obvious to them. It was Allah's gift to their *fitra* (فطرة , innate nature); it was in their genes.

Once man comprehends the message of tawhîd, he sees the one connecting factor in everything and it ends his confusion. Thereafter he will always connect the cause and the effect of events. He will have contentment because he perceives meaning in events. The seeker who has had a taste or a glimpse of the fact that which he sees outside of him is also inside him, is helped until he discovers this phenomenon in every aspect of existence. He becomes more confirmed in the science of tawhîd and thereby moves closer to the real awakening in his heart.

The majority of people who say that they believe in Allah and the Prophet Muhammad, *sallah-Ilãhu 'alayhi wa ãlihi wa sallam*, are hopeful believers. They have consciously put themselves in a situation where real belief is likely to occur. They say: *ashhadu an la ilaha illa-Ilah wa ashhadu anna Muhammadan rasulu-Ilah* (اشهدان لا اله الا الله واشهد ان محمد رسول الله). They have accepted the hypothesis. The proof of it will only come when belief is actually experienced. The path is about Allah and nothing changes this. The purpose of creation is to enter into belief. Nothing is wrong with action in the world provided it does not cause harm, but rather leads one closer to higher knowledge.

Once one comes to know the laws that govern creation, nothing comes as a surprise. No event is bewildering anymore because the essence of 'peace of mind', that is already ingrained in man, has been brought to consciousness. Man does not like to be disturbed unnecessarily or unjustly. The natural laws themselves are, in fact, a continuum of action and reaction. They are one ripple after another, one cause leading to another effect.

The nature of this world is to be in upheaval, and if you do not recognize the basis upon which the final revelation to mankind descended in its complete form, you will be in continual upheaval. The nature of Reality that is beaming within man makes him desire to be timeless, eternal, forever-living, ever-sustaining, ever-independent. These are attributes of God. If he acts according to his capacity, why should he be afflicted with upheaval? The nature of *dunyã* (دنيا , world in a negative material sense) is to repeatedly be torn like the house of the spider. There is no end to the dynamic rise and fall of the movement of events.

No bird has ever gone up but that it has come down. No one gains affection but that soon he gains hatred. No one builds a house and family but that he loses them. If he does not lose them during his life, he will lose them at his death---this is the cycle. Man has come to die. Experiencing death in the now is the final and absolute confirmation of the message of submission. If man submits to it totally, he finds nothing wrong with the secondary reality or that which has come from Reality.

If man does not submit, he finds anger and disappointment within himself. It is an expression of ignorance of existence. He wants to make the rules of this world, but because he is not God, he cannot. The *dîn* tells him to stop his anger now because its nature is fire. One does not simply suppress anger allowing it to manifest later. Anger is suppressed in the hope that the reason for the anger will be reflected upon.

وَمَا كُنتَ تَتْلُوا مِن قَبْلِهِ مِن كِتَٰبٍ وَلَا تَخُطُّهُ
بِيَمِينِكَ إِذًا لَّارْتَابَ الْمُبْطِلُونَ

48 **And you did not recite before it any book, nor did you transcribe one with your right hand, for then could those who say untrue things have doubted.**

The Prophet, *sallah-llãhu 'alayhi wa ãlihi wa sallam*, did not copy anything. He could not physically read that which came before through other prophets. He was an orphaned desert boy who, early on in his life, had cared for his own existential needs. But he was endowed with discrimination and soon realized that the ways to knowledge existing around him were actually ways of transgression and loss, so he avoided them. Then, through the purest of hearts, the tree of knowledge bore fruit within him and gave provision to everyone around him. Outwardly, he did not have access to historical information and knowledge that came before him, but in his breast he had the heart of a man of knowledge able to contain the final glorious message to mankind.

Following the Prophet, sallah-llãhu 'alayhi wa ãlihi wa sallam, is the path of Islam. If is a pure, easy and direct path, if one does not complicate it by intellectualizing. If one claims to follow in the Prophet's footsteps then it is up to him to cleanse his breast of debris and make it available to receive that which it is fit for, the root of which is already there in its *fitra*. Guidance does not come from outside. Allah permeates everything: He is *Muhit* (المحيط, the All-Encompassing). Anything in man's breast which he considers important, is an idol, and clearing it from the heart facilitates the growth of original, innate knowledge.

بَلْ هُوَ ءَايَٰتٌۢ بَيِّنَٰتٌ فِى صُدُورِ ٱلَّذِينَ أُوتُوا۟ ٱلْعِلْمَ ۚ
وَمَا يَجْحَدُ بِـَٔايَٰتِنَآ إِلَّا ٱلظَّٰلِمُونَ

49 **Nay! these are clear communications in the breasts of those who are granted knowledge; and none deny Our communications except the unjust.**

وَقَالُوا۟ لَوْلَآ أُنزِلَ عَلَيْهِ ءَايَٰتٌ مِّن رَّبِّهِۦ ۖ قُلْ إِنَّمَا ٱلْءَايَٰتُ
عِندَ ٱللَّهِ وَإِنَّمَآ أَنَا۠ نَذِيرٌ مُّبِينٌ

50 **And they say: Why are not signs sent down upon him from his Lord? Say: The signs are only with Allah, and I am only a plain warner.**

The message of Reality is clear in the heart of those who are granted knowledge. Everyone has the potential of being granted this knowledge. But the potential has to be cultivated like a seed. The seed of ignorance is easily nourished because the lower nature of man is to be at a loss—*inna-l-insana lafi khusr* (ان الانسان لفی خسر) "surely man is at a loss." To know how to nourish the seed of knowledge so that it grows is the purpose of existence. And it comes to man spontaneously by his willingness to dissociate from other-than-Allah.

اَوَلَمْ يَكْفِهِمْ اَنَّآ اَنْزَلْنَا عَلَيْكَ الْكِتٰبَ يُتْلٰى عَلَيْهِمْ ؕ اِنَّ فِىْ ذٰلِكَ لَرَحْمَةً وَّذِكْرٰى لِقَوْمٍ يُّؤْمِنُوْنَ

51 **Is it not enough for them that We have revealed to you the Book which is recited to them? Most surely there is mercy in this and a reminder for a people who believe.**

"Is it not enough for them that We have revealed to you the Book?" It is as though man has evolved to such a point that he does not need miraculous outer events to shake him out of his lethargy in order to listen to the one and only message. The Prophet had one tool, one miracle. He could talk of Reality and be understood by everyone. Other prophets came with visible openings to jolt men out of their lethargy. It was relatively clumsy but easily understood.

The miracle of Islam was that the Prophet could talk about the nature of Reality in all its aspects through his own voice which was like that of other men, bringing about a measure of familiarity and contentment to those around him. Merely seeing somebody like themselves living according to the revelation gave them great encouragement. That is the supreme miracle of Islam. The Prophet, *salla-ll ahu 'alayhi wa ãlihi wa sallam*, some of the *sahaba* and the *Ahl ul-Bayt* had the power to perform miracles, but this was not emphasized. It was not what the Prophet came with. The message of *tawhîd* was used as the spearhead of attack against the *nafs* and ignorance.

The one who has knowledge of the message of the Qur'ãn uses it like a doctor uses his knowledge, giving it to everyone who needs a cure or who is able to take it to another village to cure other people. There is also specialized knowledge for individualized treatment. When the doctor sees that a patient's heart is jammed and unable to move, he must, by the grace of Allah, produce a miracle. The miracle of miracles is to demonstrate to the patient *tawhîd*, the oneness behind multiplicity. The followers in the footsteps of the Prophet, the Imams, *awliya* , and *salihun* (صالحون , doers of good), may have appeared to perform miracles, but it was for their patients. These manifestations were odd phenomena and are not to be dwelled upon.

قُلْ كَفٰى بِاللّٰهِ بَيْنِىْ وَبَيْنَكُمْ شَهِيْدًا ج يَعْلَمُ مَا فِى
السَّمٰوٰتِ وَالْاَرْضِ ط وَالَّذِيْنَ اٰمَنُوْا بِالْبَاطِلِ وَكَفَرُوْا
بِاللّٰهِ لا اُولٰٓئِكَ هُمُ الْخٰسِرُوْنَ

52 **Say: Allah is sufficient as a witness between me and you; He knows what is in the heavens and the earth. And (as for) those who believe in the falsehood and disbelieve in Allah, these it is that are the losers.**

For the Prophet, *sallah-llãhu 'alayhi wa ãlihi wa sallam,* and those who believe in his message, it is enough that Allah is a witness between them. They believe with certainty in their hearts in the all-encompassing mercy of Allah and have abandoned themselves into its ever-flowing river of light. That certainty brings about enough joy and contentment to suffice them. They do not care for the doubts nor for the afflictions of others. Those who are at a loss, who have not found the subtle way of tuning themselves into the right path, are following a way that can only lead to a dead end. The believer looks forward to the ultimate freedom from the chains of this *dunya* (دنيا). He is looking forward to the final call that is signified by the experience of death. The person who does not have enough certainty in his heart, clings onto what he has invested in and what he knows of this world.

وَيَسْتَعْجِلُونَكَ بِالْعَذَابِ ۚ وَلَوْلَا أَجَلٌ مُّسَمًّى لَّجَاءَهُمُ الْعَذَابُ ۚ وَلَيَأْتِيَنَّهُم بَغْتَةً وَهُمْ لَا يَشْعُرُونَ

53 **And they ask you to hasten on the chastisement; and had not a term been appointed, the chastisement would certainly have come to them; and most certainly it will come to them all of a sudden while they perceive not.**

يَسْتَعْجِلُونَكَ بِالْعَذَابِ وَإِنَّ جَهَنَّمَ لَمُحِيطَةٌ بِالْكَافِرِينَ

54 **They ask you to hasten on the chastisement, and most surely hell encompasses the unbelievers;**

يَوْمَ يَغْشَٰهُمُ الْعَذَابُ مِن فَوْقِهِمْ وَمِن تَحْتِ أَرْجُلِهِمْ
وَيَقُولُ ذُوقُوا مَا كُنتُمْ تَعْمَلُونَ

55 **On the day when the chastisement shall cover them from above them, and from beneath their feet; and He will say: Taste what you did.**

The ignorant ones whose hearts are set and almost dead, ask: Where are the miracles? If bad deeds have destructive effects, where is the chastisement? Why does it not happen now? Reward or punishment is not necessarily immediately noticed. There could be a subtle time-delay factor. A man who is given to a great deal of anger and agitation may not feel the reaction of his behavior for a few days, but eventually it will manifest in the form of an ulcer or some other illness. It takes time for it to set.

An example in the political arena is the faded economic glory of the British Empire which was built upon the colonial subjugation of millions upon millions of people. Now the effects of what they did are rebounding on them. The reaction to the unjust and selfish treatment of their subjects has taken decades if not centuries to show its direct effect upon them, economically and morally.

Jahannam (جهنم), the big fire, the eternal state of affliction, is already surrounding those who are not tuning themselves to the state of *îmãn*. One does not readily notice the fire one kindles by incorrect actions because of one's limited perception and understanding. However, on the day of resurrection, on the day of reckoning where there is no possibility of personal interpretations or excuses, the fire that man has invested in during this life is so all-encompassing, that the man of denial sees nothing other than it surrounding him on every side. In this life man thinks he can escape it through one channel or another. On the next level of consciousness there is absolutely no escape.

يٰعِبَادِىَ الَّذِيْنَ اٰمَنُوْٓا اِنَّ اَرْضِىْ وَاسِعَةٌ فَاِيَّاىَ
فَاعْبُدُوْنِ

56 **O My servants who believe! surely My earth is vast, therefore Me alone should you serve.**

كُلُّ نَفْسٍ ذَآئِقَةُ الْمَوْتِ قف ثُمَّ اِلَيْنَا تُرْجَعُوْنَ

57 **Every soul must taste of death, then to Us you will be returned.**

Existentially, the believer in Allah is afflicted, tested and often opposed by his own people, as were the early adherents to the Muhammadi message. If effectively overcoming this opposition in his homeland is not possible, the way out of the affliction is to leave. A point is reached in his life where he cannot bear the extent and depth of opposition surrounding him; he reaches his limit. Then a new energy sets in as he moves in a direction toward more conducive grounds. The whole creation belongs to Allah.

If there is tyranny in a situation where one is not given the opportunity to live according to the path of truth and îmãn, then one should search for another place of dwelling. This applies to one's family, community and nation. It has been the practice of all the prophets and those who follow them: seeking until one can strengthen one's understanding and knowledge of Reality and discovering where one can benefit others who are striving towards the same goal.

The meaning of death is in every heart. If man were to truly, absolutely and fearlessly submit, then it would be very easy to experience. In this creation man experiences the good and the bad, the sour and the sweet, health and illness, and in the same way he will experience the opposite to the life-line upon which he is hanging. He will experience death which at this moment in life is only a concept.

A similarity may be recognized in the mini-death of sleep. Final and absolute separation of *rûh* (روح , spirit) from the body will take place, and there will be no possibility of return to the body. At the point of death man will know that he has returned to the ultimate foundation. In other words, he will know the meaning of *thumma ilayna turja'un* (ثم الينا ترجعون), "then to us you return." He is already in Allah by Allah, but he may not recognize it fully; he may not always spontaneously be aware of it. Everyone will come to know that he has returned to Allah, that he is not separate from Allah. This is an all-encompassing law, governing all mankind. At the point of death, he will suddenly realize that he has fallen into Allah's web, which encompasses all other webs of experiences and creations.

For the *mu'min*, his return, his death, is a continuation of his life. He has already recognized in this life that he is acting by Allah. But the *raj'a* (رجعة , return) that Allah refers to is an absolute and final one. The man of *îmãn* takes this *ãya* as his ultimate security when afflicted by the wind of opposition and doubt. The *mu'min's* death is the beginning of the next awakening. His capital and strength at the point of death is what he will have invested in life, according to the purity of his actions based on his intentions. Allah says: "Everyone will meet the face of Allah." The *mu'min* wants to see it now. His desire for this goal is measured by the extent of his abandonment of actions emanating from his selfish and lower motives.

If a man's actions in this life are not motivated by fear, anxiety, disappointment, love or hate, then his actions are purely and simply inspired. The reactions to those actions are not going to afflict him. He is closer to the knowledge of Allah here and now. Ultimately, a point comes when he experiences life and death simultaneously. From then on, the physical death is for him, only a natural phenomenon which is hardly of any consequence. This is what the sufis call *fana' fi-llah* (فناء فى الله, obliteration of the self in Allah). It is a state of awareness that keeps one constantly in remembrance that at any moment he may die.

Thus death and life become familiar to the one who has experienced *fana' fi-llah*. He recognizes that both emanate from one source and that source is Allah. He goes beyond the opposites. The ordinary man who has not tasted his death has to wait. He will also come to know that behind the opposites is Allah and his return is to Allah—*inna li-llahi wa inna ilayhi raji'un:* "We are by Allah and to Allah we return" (انا لله وانا اليه راجعون). Man is supported by Allah, sustained by the one and only Reality which manifests mercy in the form of outward sustenance.

Fanã' (فناء) is a phenomenon that is within duality. Man talks in a discriminating capacity about something that is connected with oneness. In oneness there is no discrimination. In the garden, Sayyidna Adam, *'alayhi-s-salãm*, did not know the meaning of a lie so he did not discern who *shaytan* (شيطان , satan) was. He had not experienced lies because he was the first of human creation. When *shaytan* spoke to him he believed that what he heard was the truth. He did not know the opposite of truth just as we do not know death.

The taste of *fanã'* is ingrained in man's genes. It is not some-thing that he will attain but something he will gain by ridding himself of everything that is other than Allah, by dislodging himself from what he considers to be real or solid. He will attain it by extracting himself from the spider's web he has woven of habits and patterns: the way he reacts, the way he sits, the way he eats. To taste annihilation the seeker must be willing to let go of what he has.

Correcting oneself is by knowing the bounds and knowing how one has arrived at where one is. Observing oneself objectively will immediately liberate one's next actions. They will be neutral actions which will move from bitterness to sweetness. The process is natural. The change does not occur immediately. The human being first has to stop his wrong actions and then enter into a condition of neutrality. Only then can the next stage develop naturally.

وَالَّذِينَ ءَامَنُوا وَعَمِلُوا الصَّلِحَتِ لَنُبَوِّئَنَّهُم مِّنَ الْجَنَّةِ غُرَفًا
تَجْرِى مِن تَحْتِهَا الْأَنْهَرُ خَلِدِينَ فِيهَا نِعْمَ أَجْرُ الْعَمِلِينَ

58 **And (as for) those who believe and do good, We will certainly give them abode in the high places in gardens beneath which rivers flow, abiding therein; how good the reward of the workers:**

The more man acts *fi sabili-llah*, the more he ceases to act for himself; thus, he is freer of the fire of disappointments and is more apt to be in the garden. Man is in either one of two states: happiness or sadness, contentment or discontentment, relaxation or tension, security or insecurity, love or hate. As an active being he has to be in one or more of these states according to various degrees. The less there is of hate in his heart the more there is of love. The more he is fulfilled, the less empty he is.

Ramadãn (رمضان , month of fasting) is clothed by physical emptiness, leading to inward cleansing. One starts by physically limiting oneself in order to achieve inner freedom. Outer purification will lead to inner purification. For the common Muslim, *Ramadãn* is limiting the intake of food and drink. For the discriminating Muslim, it is prohibiting the senses from anything that is undesirable. For the true *mu'min*, it is focusing the heart upon Allah and nothing else but Him. Acting in goodness for the purpose of purification will give the believer a taste of the garden. The breadth of that taste will be according to the purity of his intention.

The rivers that nourish the trees of the garden are not visible. They are underground and hidden. The state of the garden receives nourishment invisibly from the rivers of *haqiqa*. The rivers of *shari'a* are clear. Knowing how to make a garden blossom in this life in all its aspects, in all its dynamic interconnectedness, can be applied to the inward. There is a gardener in everyone. If man knows how the ecology of the garden works, it is more likely that he will see the overall ecology that sustains him. This is the original motive for scientific research.

الَّذِينَ صَبَرُوا وَعَلَىٰ رَبِّهِمْ يَتَوَكَّلُونَ

59 **Those who are patient, and on their Lord do they rely.**

وَكَأَيِّن مِّن دَابَّةٍ لَّا تَحْمِلُ رِزْقَهَا اللَّهُ يَرْزُقُهَا وَإِيَّاكُمْ
وَهُوَ السَّمِيعُ الْعَلِيمُ

60 **And how many a living creature that does not carry its sustenance: Allah sustains it and yourselves; and He is the Hearing, the Knowing.**

وَلَئِن سَأَلْتَهُم مَّنْ خَلَقَ السَّمٰوٰتِ وَالْأَرْضَ وَ سَخَّرَ
الشَّمْسَ وَالْقَمَرَ لَيَقُولُنَّ اللّٰهُ ۚ فَأَنّٰى يُؤْفَكُونَ

61 **And if you ask them, Who created the heavens and the earth and made the sun and the moon subservient, they will certainly say, Allah. Whence are they then turned away?**

When one does not immediately see the benefit of one's work, one must trust that the time needed for inner growth is not the same as that for outer growth. One may not recognize any inner openings for a long time and then suddenly perceive a quantum movement forward. Patience, as far as spiritual progress is concerned, is a necessary condition. It is the foundation upon which everything is built.

Outwardly, there is a limit to patience. Having planted a plant in the ground, one may find that it does not grow, and after six months the growing season has come and gone. The gardener who knows would pull it to examine the roots, and might find them rotten. He was impatient for the plant to grow, but because he acted from knowledge his judgement was correct.

One cannot accurately judge inner progress in relation to physical time. The effects of previous actions might take twenty years to neutralize. It is like a well that is being dug, and there is no sign of water and no encouragement that there might be a real spring beneath the ground until perhaps the last two centimeters when the water suddenly appears. That is the meaning of patience; perseverance is necessary until water is struck. Through the intensity of one's devotion and abandonment, under the guidance of a true teacher, one may be able to overcome one's past more quickly. Successfully doing this will be according to the degree of one's true submission.

"And how many a living creature that does not carry its sustenance." Man, the highest of creation, need not have anxiety about his provision. Animals do not, nor do they carry their provisions on their backs. They move from one pasture to another, roam and are nourished and sustained as they grow. They move, act and do their best, and the generous Reality provides. But creation is of a dual nature and an effort must be made, the palm tree must be shaken. For man, however, the more he accumulates, the more he uses a backup in the form of wealth and possessions, the greater is the possibility of his forgetting his true security and dependence upon Allah. He arrogantly depends on something else.

Everything has come from Allah. There is nothing wrong with gold and money, but accumulating them requires an investment of time and heart. Investing in them makes man dependent on them. The fault is not in the gold itself, for by it the quality of human life may be enhanced, but in the attachment to it.

The promise of the Creator regarding spiritual evolution is that everyone will evolve into a state of absolute dependence on Reality and complete efficiency in his functionings in this life. That dependence, that *tawakkul*, expressed by *hasbun Allahu wa ni'ma-l-wakil* (حسبنا الله ونعم الوكيل , Allah is sufficient and the best of Guardians), and *la hawla wa la quwata illa billah* (لاحول ولا قوة الا بالله, no power and no strength except in Allah), will bring about a situation in which an individual spontaneously knows how to obtain whatever he wants. He will then be free to perceive meanings.

The strong *mu'min* is better than the weak *mu'min*. The *mu'min* who has access to wealth is more useful to his neighbors and society than the *mu'min* who does not, and who only sits with a *tasbih* (تسبيح , prayer beads) in the corner of a mosque. That man has saved himself but he has done nothing for others.

Man can conceptually understand that there is one source from which everything emanates, one cause from which all effects arise. The fear of provision, the fear of not living well, the fear of not having a positive outer environment, are very critical in man's progress toward submission, and his spiritual evolution. Man generally has fear of provision. What matters is the degree to which that fear enslaves him. If he allows it to justify his actions then it is in control. But the fact that it can be talked about means that the fear is understood.

Seeking provision may be positive in that it tests man, spurring him on to positive actions. He obtains the true means of sustenance when he has turned away from the world, genuinely, in his heart and not simply by his actions. Man is accountable for whatever comes into his hands. He should not throw things away. 'Ali, *'alayhi-s-salãm*, said: What is *halal* (حلال , lawful) you are accountable for and what is *haram* (حرام , forbidden) you are punished for.

اَللّٰهُ يَبۡسُطُ الرِّزۡقَ لِمَنۡ يَّشَآءُ مِنۡ عِبَادِهٖ وَيَقۡدِرُلَهٗ ؕ
اِنَّ اللّٰهَ بِكُلِّ شَىۡءٍ عَلِيۡمٌ

62 **Allah makes abundant the means of subsistence for whom He pleases of His servants, and straitens them for whom (He pleases) surely Allah is Cognizant of all things.**

وَلَئِنۡ سَاَلۡتَهُمۡ مَّنۡ نَّزَّلَ مِنَ السَّمَآءِ مَآءً فَاَحۡيَا بِهِ
الۡاَرۡضَ مِنۡۢ بَعۡدِ مَوۡتِهَا لَيَقُوۡلُنَّ اللّٰهُ ؕ قُلِ الۡحَمۡدُ لِلّٰهِ ؕ
بَلۡ اَكۡثَرُهُمۡ لَا يَعۡقِلُوۡنَ

63 **And if you ask them Who is it that sends down water from the clouds, then gives life to the**

earth with it after its death, they will certainly say, Allah. Say: All praise is due to Allah. Nay, most of them do not understand.

Fear of provision is very deep and everyone is tested by it. Those who are involved in business will often find that eighty percent of their income comes from twenty percent of their activity. Often provision comes from where one is not looking. This is true for material wealth as well as spiritual wealth. It is proof of how clumsy man is and how subtle Reality is. Opening up one's heart to the wonderment of this existence, wandering in the garden of this creation in complete trust, utter submission and humility brings joy as a by-product.

There are many traditions describing how Allah's love for His creation manifests by withholding as well as by giving. Allah gives and then withholds in order to see whether the slave will continue to be in praise. Allah says: "You plot and I plot and I am the best of plotters." Allah's plot is to enable man to break through the plot that he has woven around himself, thinking that he has made a safe abode. Allah's plot is to purify the degree of man's îmãn and trust. The more man moves on the path, the subtler are the tests so that the individual may see the real extent of his trust.

When man thinks he is safe, that safety will be shattered if Allah loves him. Trust in Allah can develop after only a few days, or because he thinks His love is remote it could develop only after years. It is nothing other than the love of Allah that withholds his provision from him in order that he can see himself frightened, jolted and disturbed. It is then that he has to be steadfast, doing his utmost at all times. If in discussions you were always right then you would learn nothing. It is at the moment when one realizes that one is wrong that one learns. It is the love of Allah if there is provision, and it is the love of Allah if there is no provision. Allah's perfect love manifests in His laws that govern this existence. His consistent love manifests in these unchanging laws.

وَمَا هٰذِهِ الْحَيٰوةُ الدُّنْيَآ اِلَّا لَهْوٌ وَّلَعِبٌ ؕ وَاِنَّ الدَّارَ
الْاٰخِرَةَ لَهِيَ الْحَيَوَانُ ۘ لَوْ كَانُوْا يَعْلَمُوْنَ

64 **And this life of the world is nothing but a sport and a play; and as for the next abode, that most surely is the life — did they but know!**

فَاِذَا رَكِبُوْا فِي الْفُلْكِ دَعَوُا اللّٰهَ مُخْلِصِيْنَ لَهُ الدِّيْنَ
فَلَمَّا نَجّٰهُمْ اِلَى الْبَرِّ اِذَا هُمْ يُشْرِكُوْنَ

65 **So when they ride in the ships they call upon Allah, being sincerely obedient to Him, but when He brings them safe to the land, then they associate others (with Him);**

لِيَكْفُرُوْا بِمَآ اٰتَيْنٰهُمْ وَلِيَتَمَتَّعُوْا فَسَوْفَ يَعْلَمُوْنَ

66 **Thus they become ungrateful for what We have given them, so that they may enjoy; but they shall soon know.**

اَوَلَمْ يَرَوْا اَنَّا جَعَلْنَا حَرَمًا اٰمِنًا وَّيُتَخَطَّفُ النَّاسُ مِنْ
حَوْلِهِمْ ؕ اَفَبِالْبَاطِلِ يُؤْمِنُوْنَ وَبِنِعْمَةِ اللّٰهِ يَكْفُرُوْنَ

67 **Do they not see that We have made a sacred territory secure, while men are carried off by force from around them? Will they still believe in the falsehood and disbelieve in the favor of Allah?**

وَمَنْ اَظْلَمُ مِمَّنِ افْتَرٰى عَلَى اللّٰهِ كَذِباً اَوْ كَذَّبَ
بِالْحَقِّ لَمَّا جَآءَهٗ ۚ اَلَيْسَ فِىْ جَهَنَّمَ مَثْوًى لِّلْكٰفِرِيْنَ

68 **And who is more unjust than one who forges a lie against Allah, or gives the lie to the truth when it has come to him? Will not in hell be the abode of the unbelievers?**

Life on earth is like a mirage or a play that does not last. It is not dependable nor is it built upon a firm foundation. Life is flimsy like the house of the spider, perishing and then being recreated. Man's abode of worth is that state or situation which allows him to sit quietly—*'āqil* (عاقل , in full possession of one's mental capabilities)—his thoughts being tied, reflecting on the fact that what is beyond time is within him. Once a momentary glimpse of this is captured through the experience of momentary death, his boat begins to sail on the ocean of knowledge.

"So when they ride in the ships they call upon Allah." Whenever man is disturbed, he has to physically abandon into the disturbance. When he is on a ship or in a hurricane, when everything is shattered, when all his relationships have been broken, when he has no home or country, when nobody wants him, he will quite naturally call upon the power of the invisible. But once some sort of tangible help appears, once an anchor has been dropped, then the self arises and man forgets.

When man has nothing or is in trouble it is much easier for him to depend upon Allah. Even if he only has a small possession it is much more difficult to remember. It is for that reason that the sufi says the path is much easier for those who have everything and do not care for it, who have access to everything and do not find it interesting or satisfactory.

The path of truth is very difficult for those who have little and desire more. These people invest most of their lives to pay for their little houses, their monuments. When their houses get scratched, their hearts are scratched. But a person who could have owned the whole world finds no use for it. He is not interested because he knows that he can only digest one or two meals a day and that he can only sleep on one bed at a time. Those in the middle are at a loss and they are the majority--- *aktharahum la ya' qilûn* (اكثرهم لا يعقلون , most of them do not understand). This is why the majority of the people of heart resent the bourgeois existence. It is not a political doctrine, it is a spiritual one.

Muhammad, *sallah-llãhu 'alayhi wa ãlihi wa sallam*, had been promised all kinds of material gifts by his tribe if, in return, he would abandon the message. The social structure of Makkah was threatened because it was based on superstition, tyranny and accumulating wealth, like the banking-financial system of today (it is the real government). If one turns away from it, not wanting a loan or a bank account, then one becomes the biggest threat to the system.

The rebel protesting in the street is no threat. On the contrary, he is caught in the system itself. So long as the system is there and so long as he cannot have it, he will want to destroy it. The way to be free of it is to get it out of the heart. In recognizing its evil man can turn away, in a positive manner, to build a system that will enable him, his offspring and his friends, to taste joy. If one first collapses the tent of materialism in one's heart then one will find that the *kufr* (كفر , denial) system is also on its way towards collapse. Energy will be saved and one's actions will bring about positiveness. One also will find more people who are awake.

وَالَّذِينَ جَاهَدُوا فِينَا لَنَهْدِيَنَّهُمْ سُبُلَنَا ۚ وَإِنَّ اللَّهَ
لَمَعَ الْمُحْسِنِينَ

69 **And (as for) those who strive hard for Us, We will most certainly guide them in Our ways; and Allah is most surely with the doers of good.**

The way to polish the *nafs*, the way to drop off the layers of arrogance and self-importance, is through *jihăd*, striving at all times. When the *nafs* is first revealed to the seeker, the struggle is very tiring because the *nafs* is rebellious. Later on he finds that he thrives on exposing the *nafs* because it polishes the mirror. At first, the mirror has many layers of dust on it. Scraping it is hard work. Later on, polishing it is as easy as lightly passing a cloth over it. The seeker desires the light because he sees the benefit of it. Suddenly he is the reflector of Reality. His heart reflects the truth.

Striving at all times is unavoidable. No one is spared struggle because life is based entirely upon movement and dynamism—that is how time is experienced. At all times one strives more and more, harder and harder, and as a result, one finds that the afflictions become subtler and subtler. Everyone is completely caught in a web which manifests in time because man is a creature suspended in time whose essence is beyond time. He has come from a Reality which encompasses here and beyond, beginning and end, manifestation and non-manifestation, life and death.

In order to resonate and vibrate that knowledge, in order to reflect that knowledge in his own small reflector, man must abandon into the complete solid web in which he is caught and from which there is no escape. If he has completely and utterly abandoned into it then that web itself will resonate him; then he is the hand of Allah, the eye of Allah, the tongue of Allah, and then he moves by the mercy and grace of Allah. He has unified. He has directly, experientially abandoned into *tawhîd*.

The path is abandonment with the use of '*aql*, with the use of one's faculties that have been invigorated by the mercy and grace of life. There is no separation, there is only oneness. Once one has begun to act with nothing of himself interfering in the action, then he is nourished by the stream of bliss, which is the same stream as that of the pure garden. All the potential impurities that exist in this life are shed and he enters a new phase of experience.

(٥٥) سورة الرحمن مدنية
وآياتها ثمان وسبعون

SURAT UR-RAHMAN

THE BENEFICENT

Introduction

This *sûra* is attributed to the early *Makkan* period. There is a tradition related to the Prophet, *salla-llãhu 'alayhi wa ãlihi wa sallam*, in which he says: "For everything there is a bride, and the bride of the Qur'ãn is *sûrat ur-Rahmãn*." It is the only sûra which begins with a divine name. It contains aspects and contrasting parts of creation in pairs: visible man and invisible *jinn;* heaven and earth; land and sea; happiness and wretchedness. All are signs and effects emanating from the one Cause.

بِسْمِ اللَّهِ الرَّحْمَٰنِ الرَّحِيمِ

In the Name of Allah, the Beneficent, the Merciful.

الرَّحْمَٰنُ

1 **The Beneficent God,**

عَلَّمَ الْقُرْآنَ

2 **Taught the Qur'ãn.**

خلَقَ الإِنسَانَ

3 **He created man,**

عَلَّمَهُ الْبَيَانَ

4 **Taught him the clear evidence.**

Ar-Rahmãn (الرحمان , the Merciful) is one of the key attributes of Allah. Every attribute is an *ãya* (آية), a sign indicating the oneness of Allah. Everything in creation is permeated with and connected to Him.

In order for the *rahma* (رحمة , mercy) of the *Rahmãn* to be understood, appreciated and experienced, knowledge has been given to man. One cannot understand something unless it is experienced. The most valuable knowledge in life's journey is the knowledge of the Qur'ãn. Man's link to God is through the Qur'ãn, through the Book, through the knowledge that will enable him to see the all-encompassing mercy. The meaning of the *hadîth* (حديث , tradition) that Muhammad, *salla-llãhu 'alayhi wa ãlihi wa sallam* (صلى الله عليه وآله وسلم, peace and blessings be upon him and his family), was created before the creation of Adam, is that the light of the path existed before Adam. After the Qur'ãn, man, *bani Ãdam* (بنو آدم), was created. So knowledge—the light of Islam, the light of the Qur'ãn — existed before *khalaqa-l-insãn* (خلق الانسان, He created man).

The Creat or contains the knowledge of what He will create. The highest creation is the Muhammadi being, the perfect being. The knowledge of this final product, the ultimate being, the *khalîfa* (خليفه , deputy) of Allah, was with the one and only Knower, with the *'Alîm* (العليم). The light of Muhammad was there when Adam was still between water and clay. The purpose of creation was to create the perfect man, the last of the prophets, the one after whom nothing new could be added.

Every aspect of the Creation has the label of the Creator on it. Creation is in His name. By His decree His *rahma* is manifested as the knowledge of the Qur'ãn. His *rahma* then becomes the creational act—*khalaqa-l-insãn*—making wider ripples through the 'evidence'. *Bayãn* (بيان) is the clear evidence which emanates from what is most subtle, penetrating the gross physical manifestations towards which man orients his perception. This is the knowledge of witnessing. Everything that is seen bears witness to the cause of its creation and to its being subject to the decree of the Beneficent.

The knowledge of the Qur'ãn is the knowledge of *tawhîd* (توحيد , divine unity). In this instance, *rahma* may also mean the tawhîd of the *Wãhid*, the One (الواحد). Access to Him is through the knowledge of His decree, which is the Book. Creation took place according to the decree. The *bayãn* is an outcome of the nature of that creation.

Man seeks evidence for everything. He is always seeking knowledge. He seeks to know the cause, effect and proof of things. Nothing is haphazard, everything leaves its trace. Man is the trace of the Creator; he is His evidence. Everything in His existence is an *ayatu-llah* (آية الله , sign of Allah). If man knows himself, then he has known the meaning of guardianship or lordship, *rubûbiyya* (ربوبية). *Man 'arafa nafsahu fa-qad 'arafa rabbahu.* "He who knows himself has known his Lord" (من عرف نفسه فقد عرف ربه , *hadîth*).

اَلشَّمْسُ وَالْقَمَرُ بِحُسْبَانٍ

5 **The sun and the moon follow a reckoning.**

وَّالنَّجْمُ وَالشَّجَرُ يَسْجُدٰنِ

6 **And the herbs and the trees adore (Him).**

The physical vehicle of man depends upon the mixture of minerals, proteins and all other elements subtly interconnected with the entire cosmic balance. Life cannot exist without the sun. When the sun begins to disappear, life will begin to cease in its different forms, and after a short period of time will end totally. The sun is self-effulgent while the moon is a faithful reflector, though it too has its influence over life.

As Reality is self-evident, so is Allah self-evident. Reality's reflector is the Prophet, *salla-llãhu 'alayhi wa ãlihi wa sallam*. Both the sun and the moon have a beginning and an end, like the two sides of a coin. The cosmic journey had its start and will have its end. But beginning and ending have one nature — the coin is one coin. The subject is one subject but there are two aspects to it, facing each other. This is the condition of the journey in this universe; it is also the condition of the self-generating light and its reflection.

"And the herbs and the trees adore (Him)." *Najm* (نجم) means herbs or grasses, and also means a star. *Najama* (نجم) is to appear, to become clear, evident, *'Ilmu-n-nujûm* (علم النجوم) is the science of astrology, of predicting the future. *Najjãm* (نجّام) is an astrologer. *Shajar* (شجر) is a plant that has a *sãq* (ساق), a trunk or stem. The plants themselves do *sajda* (سجدة , prostration). All of creation does *sajda*---those that have a visible body supporting them and those that are creeper-like; those that have the characteristic of uprightness and those that do not; those who do *Iqãma* (اقامة), who stand up acknowledging their Creator, and those who crawl from one misery to another. Whether an entity looks dependent and is striving upwards like the *shajar* (tree), or is afloat like the *najm* (star), appearing independent, it is in prostration.

Sajada (سجده) also means to adore. Entities adore, prostrate, and are under the control of the one Reality. It makes no difference whether they are celestial entities or terrestrial entities, they are all under the *haymana* of Allah (هيمنة , guardianship or control). They are under the control of the one and only Controller—they have no option but to be in *sujûd* (سجود, prostration).

وَالسَّمَآءَ رَفَعَهَا وَوَضَعَ الْمِيزَانَ

7 **And the heaven, He raised it high, and He set up the balance,**

As part of creation the heavens are uplifted. The cosmos is expanded and the balance of its destiny has been set by *al-mîzan* (الميزان, the balance). The entire cosmic creation is based on the balancing forces that hold it together, keeping it, as well as one's inner loftiness and spirit, in dynamic flux.

Imãm Husain, *alayhi-s-salãm*, was asked about *ar-Rahmãn* in the first *ãya* of this *sûra* (سورة). He said, "The Giver of the *rûh* (روح , spirit) will also give the *rãha* (راحة, rest and comfort)." One will be given according to the extent to which he lifts himself up through the balance of *sharî'a* (شريعة) and *haqîqa* (حقيقة), the outward path and the inner truth. Everything is in balance. Balance does not only mean justice, it also means that every aspect of this creation, heavenly or otherwise, affects its opposite.

Transgression is against both oneself and everyone else, because there is no otherness. If someone unjustly destroys another human being, he symbolically destroys the entire creation, which includes himself. Every human being contains the meaning of everything. To reestablish the balance, the killer himself has to be destroyed. From the point of view of *haqîqa,* killing one thing is killing everything. As upholders of *sharî'a*, men must act accordingly; the killer's punishment is the same as his crime. Because he has destroyed himself in the meaning sense, so too must he be destroyed in the physical sense.

If love is destroyed in the meaning sense, then one had better destroy it in the physical sense and part company. If there is no love or respect between two people, it will be reflected: the inner will emerge in the outer.

Man cannot take something from one side of a balance without the other side being imbalanced. It may be so subtle that he does not see it, but nothing goes unheeded by Allah. Smallness, as far as the balancing act in creation is concerned, is as significant as bigness. Look at the size of the atom bomb compared to the destruction that it does. What is the size of love? Man is not the judge or the balancer, Allah is. He measures everything in His judgement. What is the quality of a *rûh*? Is someone's *rûh* better than someone else's?

Man expects equity which means that, potentially, everyone has the same base. He does not accept someone being placed higher than himself. There is equity but there is no equality. One fellow spends his life polishing his heart, doing good deeds, while another does not. In using his *'aql* (عقل , faculty of reason) man can understand that equality does not exist.

For example, every finger is different from every other finger. They are not equal, but there is equity among them in that they can perform similar functions. Each finger can potentially have the same effect, though each is unique. If someone builds a house while you spend your time listening to the birds, in the end you will not have a house and he will not be an expert in bird calls. Having a house is not equal to being able to distinguish bird calls, they are different. But you will accept this inequality because you have enjoyed listening to the birds. There is no equality here, but there is equity.

Spiritually, everyone has the same possibility of dying into Reality, of knowing Allah. How can anyone say that his heart is better than someone else's? There is no equality because not every potential will be realized. Not everyone will be in complete abandonment; not everyone will be pure of heart.

Man's potential is restricted within the bounds of certain circumstances. For example, a person may have only one leg as the result of an accident or birth defect. Within these bounds, however, there is no restriction in the degree to which one may abandon, the degree to which one may believe, the degree to which one may live in *ihsãn* (احسان , state of doing good deeds). During life's journey one's intentions may be increasingly purified. If this were not the case where would the *rahma* of Allah be? If there is *jabr* (جبر , predestined, inescapable decree of fate), there is no *rahma*. The *rahma* of Allah is the freedom of man's spiritual progress by his abandonment.

In this life people are either on higher or lower spiritual and material planes. This is the outcome of the interaction of man's will with the creational laws and realities, some of which he may never overcome. Someone who has lost a leg cannot grow another one. It is a limitation, but which is more important, a physical limitation or a spiritual limitation?

Through knowledge of the Book of creation, through the Qur'ãn, the *Rahmãn* has given man the possibility of rising towards Allah to the ultimate degree. Reaching this goal is by means of avoiding other-than-Allah. That is the freedom man has, otherwise he is limited. Everyone has a limitation, every prophet has a limitation, every seeker has a limitation. Where man is not limited is in the degree to which he can depend on Allah, abandon into Allah, and have no thought except of Allah and no expectation than of Allah. To unify one's destiny with Allah's will—that is freedom.

Man will sometimes accept situations that do not allow him the possibility of absolute *taqwa* (تقوى , fearful awareness), of being a true *khalîfa* (representative) of Allah, because that is the mark of his humanity. It is the Creator's mark upon man. He therefore has to strive. The path is clear. It is the path of Islam based on the knowledge of the Qur'ãn, which is the manifestation of Allah's *rahma*.

أَلَّا تَطْغَوْا فِي الْمِيزَانِ

8 **That you may not exceed in the measure.**

وَأَقِيمُوا الْوَزْنَ بِالْقِسْطِ وَلَا تُخْسِرُوا الْمِيزَانَ

9 **And keep up the balance with equity and do not make the measure deficient.**

Taghã (طغا) is to overflow, to go beyond bounds. *Taghiya* (طاغية) is a despot or tyrant. Tyranny is gross. There are many subtler forms of transgression which are more difficult to discern and which one must get rid of so that one does not cut across the laws of Reality. Allah's way is the perfect *mîzãn* (ميزان , balance), free of transgression.

Aqîmu (اقيم) is from *aqãma* (اقام), to establish, keep in order, make right. *Wazn* (وزن) is weight or the importance given to things. *Qist* (قسط) is allotment, a portion of what is due, justice, equity. Allah says that He has established the balance. As the representative of Reality, man has to be faithful to Allah, Who has established the perfect balance.

"And do not make the measure deficient." *Khasara* (خسر) is to lose. If man loses the balance he has lost himself because he has allowed the lower self to act according to its orientation of imbalance and *kufr* (كفر , denial). It is denial of the *Rahmãn*. Suddenly he finds that creation has toppled him over, leaving him no access to the purpose of creation, which is the knowledge of Qur'ãn.

One of the Imãms said: "When a man is in darkness, the Qur'ãn becomes to him like a dark tomb or derelict house: it gives him no nourishment or support." This is the case with the majority of mankind; they have lost the *mîzãn*. *Al-Mîzãn* is also the name of the Qur'ãn.

If man insures that he does not upset what is already in balance, then he is unlikely to do himself injustice. He is then closer to being a living Qur'ãn. Allah is telling man to give value to balance. Man should be concerned, conscientious, aware and in *dhikr* (ذكر , remembrance). Does he know what he is doing and why? Does he know his own intention? Are his intention and action unified? Man should question and follow his heart and 'aql as one path.

The Prophet, salla-llãhu 'alayhi wa ãlihi wa sallam, said: "Anger corrupts *îmãn* (trust, faith) as vinegar corrupts honey." Man builds things, but corrupts them because he does not give priority and importance to patience. What weight does man give to the meaning of "and do not make the measure deficient?" The balance is that which is absolutely right, Man is moving along the path from the womb to the tomb. Balance is about recognizing that one is the *barzakh* (برزخ , interspace). One is in this world but not of this world. Man has come only to go. The balance is being both here and with Allah, alive and yet, with every closing of the eye, willing to be under six feet of dust.

وَالْأَرْضَ وَضَعَهَا لِلْأَنَامِ

10 **And the earth, He has set it for living creatures;**

فِيهَا فَاكِهَةٌ وَّالنَّخْلُ ذَاتُ الْأَكْمَامِ

11 **Therein are fruit and palms having sheathed clusters,**

Allah set up the earth in order that man, who is in continuous flux and disturbance, should come to recognize his origin, to recognize how he has fallen from before time into *fitra* (فطرة,)innate character), and to recognize how he has come into being from non-being. As part of His mercy, he has been dropped into *janna* (جنّة , the garden) in the same way as his forefathers were. When Adam came out from the crack of non-time, Allah told him that this garden had been given to him so that he could have *maqarr* (مقّر , a place of stability, such as a house). Qarra (قرّ), the root of maqarr, means to settle. He who has settled admits to the mercy of the Creator. Everything points to the *Rahmãn.*

Life is characterized by motion and can only be experienced in time. When time stops, life stops. That is *al-qiyãmatu-s-saghira* (القيامة الصغيرة , the small Day of Reckoning). On that day there is no time left to change the balance of the accumulated good and bad actions. People who have come close to death through accidents and have returned, say that on the Day of Reckoning a film of one's life is played to them in a split second.

If man is to qualify for knowledge of Allah, it will be by his knowledge of the *Rahmãn*, which is attained by upholding the *mîzãn*—the Qur'ãn. Man's qualification for admittance to the *rahma* of the knowledge of the Qur'ãn is dependent upon his leaving himself behind when he enters the Qur'ãn, because the Qur'ãn is like the room of Allah: it is where Allah's laws and knowledge are kept. Man can only come to Allah with *taqwa*. He can only approach Him with abandonment and the right attitude, waiting to see the mercy, trusting that there is nothing other than the mercy of Allah, praying that he will see it manifest to him in the form of knowledge which can be transferred into behavior. That is the qualification; otherwise the study of the Qur'ãn remains "Islamic Studies." Everything goes back to Allah. Every knowledge takes man back to where it emanated from, its root and source.

Al-ard (الارض , the earth) is necessary for man and is part of the garden. *Ardiyya* (ارضية), which means foundation or ground floor, provides man—who is in continuous turmoil biologically, physiologically, mentally and spiritually—the possibility of remembering the beyond-time. In the Qur'ãn Allah says: *Alastu birabbikum* (الست بربكم); "Am I not your Lord?" By forgetting everything else, the innate, *fitrî* (فطرى) remembrance that there is only Allah will come to man. On the *ard* man is able to recognize that all the creatures fulfill their natures and have come from One Creator.

Fãkiha (فاكهة) is fruit. *Fukãha* (فكاهة) is something that is pleasant or gives amusement. Pleasures are diversions from the undesirable, bringing man tranquility and balance. The normal state of a person of abandonment is joy. But if a person has not totally abandoned into Allah, experiencing joy, then he seeks pleasures. They are things that make man less mentally agitated and fulfill his physical desires so that he begins to pay attention to his inner fulfillment.

The physical description of the garden is a *mithãl* (مثال , metaphor): the Qur'ãn indicates to man the meaning of the end by describing its pleasures. Man seeks fruit not because there is something spiritual about the fruit itself, but because he is made more spiritual after he has satisfied his appetite by it. His origin is spiritual, but he has exaggerated his physical and mental needs. When they are removed, he finds himself to be well. It is the state that the garden brings about that is important, not the detailed description of it; but there are details for every person's needs ..."and palms having sheathed clusters." The creation manifests in clusters. From the one branch come the many. Allah's mercy is abundant in every form.

Life is transient and in perpetual change and therefore unstable. How can one take man's changing moods and desires seriously? What man desires now has nothing to do with what he desired fifteen years ago. Yet he has the audacity to claim he is the same person that he was fifteen years ago. After many years his knowledge, his experiences, habits and attitudes, are all different. On the other hand, how can anyone say that he has changed if he does not recognize and admit that there is something within him that never changes? How can man get up in the morning and say that he has slept well or badly unless there is something within him that never sleeps? "Slumber does not overtake Him nor sleep." (*sûratu-l-Baqara:* 255) How can man say he has been very angry unless there is something within him that is most compassionate? What man wants most earnestly is that which is forever, *al-Bãqî* (الباقى , the Everlasting). Everyone is on that path whether he likes it or not, whether he sees it now or later.

Man has been brought to this earth to be tested as part of his *tarbiya* (تربية , upbringing). He is being brought up to recognize what is transient and what is not, what is permanent and what is not, what is meaningful and what is not. Whatever is of change is from his *nafs* (نفس, lower self). The reason man does not see the hand of Allah behind everything is that he interferes and interjects the projections of his self. If he were to put himself aside, there would only be the one and only Reality.

The fall from the state of the garden came about because of the rise of consciousness—because Adam questioned. If man desires to be in the garden he should not question, but he should make use of his *'aql*. As a result, he will receive answers to his questions. When man enters the garden in this life he does not care for the garden of the next because he has tasted it already. The desire for the garden falls from his heart. Then there is no desire except the desire to see the face of Allah in every direction towards which he turns.

وَالْحَبُّ ذُو الْعَصْفِ وَالرَّيْحَانُ

12 **And the grain with (its) husk and fragrance.**

فَبِأَيِّ آلَاءِ رَبِّكُمَا تُكَذِّبَانِ

13 **Which then of the bounties of your Lord will you deny?**

Big things come from little things. *Habb* (حب) is a seed. The literal meaning of *habb* is the seed that comes from grasses. There are many different types of vegetation and their meanings are linked to the nourishment which they provide. The living, sentient creatures and the vegetable kingdom are interdependent. The highest creature, man, depends on those that are lower because he originates from dust. Yet, he loves the higher because of its subtlety. There is something in him that always makes him love subtler meaning. The Prophet, *salla-llãhu 'alayhi wa ãlihi wa sallam*, loved prayer, perfume and women. He loved what is most subtle, the prayer, as well as what is more gross and physical, the companionship of women. Once man's physical needs are fulfilled, he seeks higher satisfaction in meanings. If man is fortunate, he reaches physical fulfillment, which then leads him to question meanings. Most people at the point of death have only achieved small, short-term, physical goals which are empty of meanings.

Wherever man looks there is the sign of the *Rahmãn*, even in what man considers to be an affliction. All events occur according to the laws that govern existence which are from the Law-Giver. Man may not like an event, but that is because of himself. What man wants will not necessarily happen, but what Allah wants will happen. If what man wants is what Allah wants, then there is perfect harmony; then he is saved. If there is disharmony, then all that man can do is to be in *Istighfãr* (استغفار , asking for forgiveness), because he has acted incongruously with Allah's laws.

Everything man considers to be a sign is actually a double sign. The fact that it was there and yet remained undiscerned by him is a sign that he was asleep. Whatever a man experiences that leads him to a new understanding that was already within him but not perceived, is because he did not have the requisite knowledge and wisdom to perceive it. Suppose someone did not know the meaning of fear until he was twenty-three, when he fell down a crevice. The meaning of fear was in his being, but he had not yet experienced it. You may not have experienced injustice, but the injustice of man has existed since the creation of Adam. With man came his injustice, which the *malã'ika* (ملائكة ,angels) were afraid would corrupt the earth. Whatever you experience, feel or think, that is your biography; it is of no interest to anybody else because it is common to all of mankind. The seeker is only interested in Allah, the Real.

Whatever a man now understands, other people have understood before him. Whatever he now perceives has been perceived by others before him, though every man will contend that he is the first to have perceived it. He follows what *Iblîs* (ابليس, satan) said: "I am better than them." It is the rise of the ego and the fall of man.

خَلَقَ الْإِنْسَانَ مِنْ صَلْصَالٍ كَالْفَخَّارِ

14 **He created man from dry clay like earthen vessels.**

وَخَلَقَ الْجَآنَّ مِنْ مَّارِجٍ مِّنْ نَّارٍ

15 **And He created the jinn of a flame of smokeless fire.**

فَبِاَيِّ اٰلَآءِ رَبِّكُمَا تُكَذِّبٰنِ

16 **Which then of the bounties of your Lord will you deny?**

Man is created from hard clay, *salsãl* (صلصال). His existential situation is based on a firm structure. Man's firmness is an echo of his subtlety. His real nourishment is of a most subtle nature. The subtlest of nourishments turns the heart when it is open, and not in desire or depression. The more open man's heart is, the more it can express that openness—as long as it is in a firm and solid container. The greater the value of a thing, the harder and the more secure its shell.

The double meaning of the signs denotes duality. Everything in existence has its mirror image. For *ins* (انس , man) there is *jinn* (جن , unseen beings). Man is the visible creature of the two. *Uns* (اُنسْ) means intimacy, solace, companionship. *Nasiya* (نَسِيَ) is also related to *ins,* and means to forget. *Nisa*' (نساء , women), from the same root, are those who make men forget Allah. The meaning of *nisã* is related to *uns*, because women do give solace.

Jinn are entities which do not manifest in a physically solid state. They are created from smokeless fire because smoke is a condensation of matter and as such has density. *Jinn* have their bounds in the same way as *ins* have theirs. Thus, there is an interface between *jinn* and man.

The *jinn* are hidden, invisible. The word *jinn* is related to *janna* (جنّة), that which is hidden, the garden whose foliage is so dense that one cannot see the ground. *Jinn* are created of smokeless fire. The subtle source of both *jinn* and *ins* is light, *nûr* (نور). "Allah is the light of the heavens and earth," (الله نور السموات, *suratu-n-Nûr*: 35). As light descends, as it becomes physicalized or as it becomes possible for it to be manifest or reflected, it takes the form of *jinn* and *ins*.

Whatever one looks at is a sign, whether *jinn* or *ins*. How can man deny these bounties? Every sign is a bounty, every sign is a provision. What man now seeks is the confidence of knowing that at all times the *Rahmãn* is behind each reflection in creation. It is said that if a Muslim reads *sûratu-r-Rahmãn* every day at *fajr* (فجر , daybreak), he will never be afflicted or, if he is afflicted in the eyes of others, he himself will only see the *rahma* of the *Rahmãn*. The reader becomes what is read: if he truly reads then he will have recognized what he has read.

Wherever one turns, there is the generosity and *ni'ma* (نعمة, blessing) of Allah. But man takes it for granted and does not recognize that all is from Allah. He forgets and becomes distracted because he connects to what is in front of him.

Because man is the highest of all creations, he has in himself the ability to tune in to different wavebands. He can tune in to *jinn* but that is a transgression and is not allowed. It is like spying on someone. If a person wants to be known, he presents himself openly. Why tune to his transmitter when his house is shut to you? A man of submission and reality, being given this gift, should use it entirely to serve Allah. *Nabiyyu-llãh* (نبي الله Prophet of Allah) Sulaimãn, *'alayhi-s-salãm*, had the power to connect with animals. When travelling with his army he could hear the ants talking of his approach.

Man cannot tolerate what goes on in his mind or in the minds of others. If he were to hear of what was going to happen to him in the future, he might wish to shoot himself. Every system has its limitations, which are at the same time its constriction and its bounty. The fact that there is the visible and the invisible is a bounty. Everything within its container is a reflection of perfection. If man accepts the limitations he can begin to reflect perfection.

رَبُّ الْمَشْرِقَيْنِ وَرَبُّ الْمَغْرِبَيْنِ

17 **Lord of the two risings and Lord of the two settings.**

فَبِأَيِّ آلَاءِ رَبِّكُمَا تُكَذِّبَانِ

18 **Which then of the bounties of your Lord will you deny?**

"Lord of the two risings and Lord of the two settings." *Gharaba* (غرب), the root of *maghribayn* (مغربين), means to go away. One of the meanings that *Amîru-l-Mu'minîn* (امير المؤمنين) 'Ali gave for this *ãya* was concerning duality, such as that of the seasons. He said: "The *shurûq* (شروق , sunrise) of winter is different from the shurûq of summer, and the *ghurûb* (غروب , sunset) of summer is different from the *ghurûb* of winter."

There is a summer and there is a winter; they both have meaning. In winter everything is dormant, while in summer life is in full bloom. The sun of winter is different from the sun of summer. 'Ali, *'alayhi-s-salãm*, also said: "Every day has its *burj* (برج ,its sign of the zodiac), and there are three hundred and sixty *burûj* (plural of *burj*), " For every day there is a new *shurûq* and a new *ghurûb*. The sun has its circuit. The rising of the sun on this life brings light, and light is only meaningful if it gives man knowledge. If there is light outside and the eyes are closed, the light is of no use.

There is a rise of consciousness both for this life and for the next. For each there is one *shurûq*, there is a coming out. This is, of course, also true of *ghurûb*. The people of "*irfãn* (عرفان ,gnosis) and *tasawwuf* (تصوّف ,sufism) often refer to the two risings as the risings of knowledge in the heart and '*aql,* and the two settings as the settings of the *nafs*. As there comes the rising of the '*aql*, reason, there is disappearance of association.

There are also risings for different creatures, the *ins* and the *jinn*, each seeing a different sun rising and setting. There can be no rising without a setting. Whatever manifests, whatever one can discern, is one side of a two-sided coin. Once there is a creational situation there are two aspects to it. At the beginning there is one, at the end there is one, and in between there are two.

مَرَجَ الْبَحْرَيْنِ يَلْتَقِيَانِ

19 **He has made the two seas to flow freely--- they meet:**

بَيْنَهُمَا بَرْزَخٌ لَّا يَبْغِيَانِ

20 **Between them is a barrier which they cannot pass.**

فَبِاَىِّ اٰلَاۤءِ رَبِّكُمَا تُكَذِّبٰنِ

21 **Which then of the bounties of your Lord will you deny?**

The two seas have met before creation and they will meet again after creation. They are two seas, one of pure water, the other of impure, salty water. The sweet water that comes from the mountains and rivers does not mix with the salt water.

The seas here are like two states that meet, the two states of wake-fulness and sleep, the two seas of sharî'a and haqîqa, the two seas of meaning and sensory. Both the physical and non-physical parts of man's life have their laws. The law of haqîqa hinges on the loyalty of abandonment, îmãn, which takes man to 'the station of *haqqu-l-yaqîn* (حق اليقين ,truth of certainty). The law of *sharî'a* holds man to the five pillars of Islam, so necessary because he is in the tempestuous sea of the sensory.

How can man deny the bounties of the two seas of the inner and the outer? They will meet as they have met before. At the point of creation they were one and at the point of death they will merge once again. In this reality, what is holding them apart is the double mercy of Allah.

For the duration of this life there is an invisible barrier, an interspace between an apparent duality that does not allow the seas to connect. In the same way, the sun and the moon follow a reckoning—*bihusbãn* (بحسبان). They came from one source and then were catapulted into space as two. Moving according to a certain complex pattern, they will eventually come together again. There is an interspace between them that holds them apart as a man's body seems to be separate from his *rûh*.

There is the *qalb* (قلب ,heart, from the root *qalaba,* to turn), and there is the *rûh*. The *rûh*, being disconnected from the world, is connected to the precreational state and can therefore give man comfort. Unlike the rûh, the *qalb* may be seized by *dunya*' (دنيا,world in a negative material sense). The heart may be damaged by the world's salty sea, and if it is, then the *rûh* in turn can no longer provide comfort. If the *nafs* is purified then the heart can freely turn. It is no longer caught in the see-saw of the *dunyã* which continues; taking breath in and letting breath out, the inhaled breath being pure air, the exhaled impure. Neither of them mix with the other. These are the *bahrayn* (بحرين), the two seas.

Everywhere one looks there are the two seas, separated by a subtle barrier. The seas of knowledge and ignorance do not mix. Life and death do not mix. Whatever man looks at, creation appears in one form or another. It is agreeable or disagreeable. A creational entity is considered to be usable or unusable. Nothing transgresses the bounds because of the *mîzãn*, the balance. Creation is not chaos, it is cosmos.

يَخۡرُجُ مِنۡهُمَا اللُّؤۡلُؤُ وَالۡمَرۡجَانُ

22 **There come forth from them pearls and coral.**

فَبِاَیِّ اٰلَآءِ رَبِّكُمَا تُكَذِّبٰنِ

23 **Which then of the bounties of your Lord will you deny?**

From the seas come the pearl and the coral. If one dives into the seas, these amazing jewels may be seen. *Jawhar* (جوهر) is jewel; it also means intrinsic nature or essence. If one wants the essence of these seas, then one must get their *jawãhir*, their jewels, but diving for these jewels is dangerous, for one risks sustaining bruises and cuts from the reef.

The formation of the pearl is an act of rejection. The material of the pearl is the secretion of the oyster used to isolate and discharge the grain of sand that has entered its body. It is the material used to disconnect, dislodge and discharge it.

Marjãn (مرجان), coral, is formed by the reverse process and is the substance within which the animal dwells. It is the structure in which the animal houses and shelters itself, and later it is left behind. So one structure is formed by repulsion, the other by attraction.

The thought process operates either by repulsion or attraction. Whatever comes to man's thoughts is either something he wants to dissociate from and forget, or something he wants to hear again and again and to which he wants to connect. Man oscillates between the two sides of the *mîzãn*, the pearl and the coral.

Every man is continuously turning between something he wants and something he does not want. The seeker loves the men of tawhîd, he loves the people who want to see Allah, and he runs from the people of *kufr* (كفر ,denial). He wants the good news that Islam is prevailing in the world. He wants to hear the good news that his children are growing up decently—and not the bad news that they have been mischievous. The human being is constantly oscillating between wanting to surround himself with what he likes, and repulsing and dissociating himself, like the oyster, from what he dislikes. The opposites grow from the same root; they are two distinct entities that have the same origin to which they will ultimately revert.

وَلَهُ الْجَوَارِ الْمُنشَآتُ فِي الْبَحْرِ كَالْأَعْلَامِ

24 **And His are the ships reared aloft in the sea like mountains.**

فَبِاَيِّ اٰلَاۤءِ رَبِّكُمَا تُكَذِّبٰنِ

25 **Which then of the bounties of your Lord will you deny?**

Both *'alãma* (علامة), meaning sign, and *'alam* (علم), meaning flag, are from the same root as *'ilm* (علم , knowledge); they imply something being known. The *munsha'at* (منشات), the root of which is *nasha'a* (نشأ , to create, to loom up) announce themselves; they are highly evident. Whatever is afloat belongs to Allah. The phenomenon of floating, as well as the entire interactional balancing scene that brings about desirable situations, such as ships on the sea, belongs to Allah.

Reflect upon how certain situations are the opposite of what someone might expect; for instance, how steel ships float upon water. The ships float because of verifiable laws easily demonstrated by scientists, but still, it is very odd. All that one sees, all of these projections of Reality, all that flickers of knowledge or experience, will ultimately disappear because they are in time.

كُلُّ مَنْ عَلَيْهَا فَانٍ

26 **Everyone on it must pass away.**

وَّيَبْقٰى وَجْهُ رَبِّكَ ذُو الْجَلٰلِ وَالْاِكْرَامِ

27 **And there endures forever the face of your Lord, the Lord of glory and honor.**

فَبِأَيِّ آلَاءِ رَبِّكُمَا تُكَذِّبَانِ

28 **Which then of the bounties of your Lord will you deny?**

Whatever is on this *ard*, whatever is physicalized, solidified, or appears to have an identity, has no identity other than Allah—*Lã ilãha illa-llãh*, there is no God but Allah. Everything announces its perishability. If it is solid—a plant or a creature—it proves its destiny. What remains is the fount of creation, *wajhu rabbika* (وجه ربک , the face of your Lord). *Wajh* (وجه) is a direction or face, the outer visible front. In his formal worship the Muslim must have *tawajjuh* (توجه , attention), and point his *wajh* towards the formal, ancient abode of safety that came about through the inspiration of Sayyidna Ibrãhîm, *'alayhi-s-salãm*, in Makkah. Whoever does *salãt* (صلاة , prayer) positions himself towards that.

All of creation honors its covenant; every creational entity honors the Most Honorable—"the Lord of glory and honor" is an attribute of Allah, the Glorious, the Most Honorable, the One Who bestows honor. Man is an honorable creature, if only he would realize it; if only he could unify his physical reality with his innate reality. Man honors his contract by physiologically perishing. Everyone honors his destiny, knowingly or not.

Man sees, contained in the facade of creation, the *af'ãl* (افعال) , the manifestation of actions. In the case of humans, they are a result of the interactions of his heart and his lower *nafs*. The less involved is his *nafs*, the more involved is his heart. Looking further inward, there is the *rûh*. If one's *nafs* has been burnt away, then his heart is active and pulsating; it is then fed by the spring of comfort—the *rûh*, the spirit.

Those who are not in submission rebel against the fact that they are perishing. If you tell someone that he is aging and that his teeth are falling out, he will say that he is not yet old or ready to die. Everyone considers his age as the average. When you were twelve years old, you thought fifty was ancient. You could not communicate with fifty-year-olds, they were funny people. But when you became fifty, you thought fifty was quite young. This is because there is in man an echo of the Everlasting.

But there is also in man an echo of the *nafs* of rebellion. He assumes that the *nafs* lasts forever, and does not remember death. The seeker is repeatedly given the advice by his masters that the most potent medicine for ailments of the spirit is the remembrance of death. It is not used to paralyze man or to make him inactive and negative but, on the contrary, it is used to make him successful in his actions by making him more efficient. If he constantly remembers death, his actions will be pure, untarnished by his personal greed, arrogance, vanity, revenge and whatever other attributes are characteristic of the lower self.

The face of the Lord is, at first, an existential connection between man and Reality. Man wants to be healthy, he wants to be in the company of fine men, he wants to be in an environment that will help him get deeper into the knowledge of Reality, of which there is no end. The more one knows Allah, the greater is the desire to know more of Allah. One should not assume that once somebody knows Allah that is the end of it. There is no beginning or end to Reality. An *'ãrif bi-llãh* (عارف بالله) is one who has had a window open onto Reality. The more he is able to look out from that window, the more he will see of Reality.

Just as each human has a physical birth, so too does each one have a spiritual awakening, which takes place parallel in time. Just as man was physically once a child, so too was he a child in knowledge of Allah. There is no end to Reality, because It encompasses before and after creation.

"And there endures forever the face of your Lord." The Qur'ãn says that the Lord's day is like a thousand years of man's time; and this reckoning is only made in relationship to the time-frame of this world. As far as its relationship to beyond this world, it is fifty thousand years. So each day is the equivalent of fifty thousand years. Time is obviously relative. A day is a period of time, and not necessarily the twenty-four hour span that is measured by the odd machine called a clock.

يَسْئَلُهُ مَنْ فِى السَّمٰوٰتِ وَالْاَرْضِ ط كُلَّ يَوْمٍ هُوَ فِى شَاْنٍ

29 **All those who are in the heavens and the earth ask of Him; every moment He is upon some affair.**

فَبِاَىِّ اٰلَاۤءِ رَبِّكُمَا تُكَذِّبٰنِ

30 **Which then of the bounties of your Lord will you deny?**

Allah is man's Lord. Lordship is the source of the emanation of action. It is sustainership. The lord of a house has to attend to every aspect of the house, every *sha'n* (شان), every business and affair. The lord of a house looks after its hardware—its maintenance and so on—as well as all the aspects of its software: the people, children and food, in the same way as the Lord of lords looks after creation. In every instant, every affair comes to Him. Lordship is attending to every affair; otherwise, there would be no *tawhîd*. *Tawhîd* is the one core from which all networks emanate, superimpose on each other and connect.

سَنَفْرُغُ لَكُمْ اَيُّهَا الثَّقَلٰنِ

31 **Soon will We apply Ourselves to you, O you two armies.**

فَبِاَيِّ اٰلَاۤءِ رَبِّكُمَا تُكَذِّبٰنِ

32 **Which then of the bounties of your Lord will you deny?**

Thaqula (ثقل) means to be weighty. *Thaqalãn* (ثقلان) means two entities or realities, seen or unseen. It can also mean two armies. *Faragha* (فرغ) means to be empty, to finish off, and here means to apply or occupy. Every *jinn* and *ins*, whether *mu'min* (believer) or *kãfir* (كافر ,denier), having either attained knowledge or remained in ignorance, will come to know the day of reckoning. Everyone knows that whatever affair he is handling will come to an end. If it does not come to an end in this world while he is still alive, it will come to an end at his personal *qiyãma* (قيامة), at the hour of his death. Man is completely and totally cornered. He has no way to escape from the prison of time. If man dies into his situation, he is enlivened by the non-time Reality which encompasses the yard of this prison. If you die into the clock, you will not hear it anymore—it will be as if gone. As far as you are concerned, there will no longer be a clock; you will have transcended it.

يٰمَعْشَرَ الْجِنِّ وَالْاِنْسِ اِنِ اسْتَطَعْتُمْ اَنْ تَنْفُذُوْا مِنْ اَقْطَارِ السَّمٰوٰتِ وَالْاَرْضِ فَانْفُذُوْا لَا تَنْفُذُوْنَ اِلَّا بِسُلْطٰنٍ

33 **O assembly of jinn and men! If you are able to pass through the regions of the heavens and the earth, then pass through; you cannot pass through but with authority.**

فَبِاَيِّ اٰلَاۤءِ رَبِّكُمَا تُكَذِّبٰنِ

34 **Which then of the bounties of your Lord will you deny?**

Qutr (قطر , plural is *aqtãr*, اقطار) is a diameter, region, zone, or something which is encompassed — a dominion. If one uses a compass, one creates a circle that encompasses a space. "If you are able to pass through the regions of the heavens and the earth, then pass through." Allah encourages man to explore, but he cannot unless he attains the power, unless he obtains the *sultãn* (سلطان ,authority). It is a positive challenge to man.

Every sphere or zone has an energy. If man wants to go beyond a zone he must be able to pierce its limit. To escape the gravitational pull of earth a missile needs to obtain the speed of 17,000 miles per hour. Man needs *sultãn* to overcome gravity. All of the powers are part of the one and only all-encompassing Power, which is an interzonal power.

يُرْسَلُ عَلَيْكُمَا شُوَاظٌ مِّنْ نَّارٍ وَّنُحَاسٌ فَلَا تَنْتَصِرٰنِ

35 **The flames of fire and smoke will be sent on you two, then you will not be able to defend yourselves.**

فَبِاَيِّ اٰلَاۤءِ رَبِّكُمَا تُكَذِّبٰنِ

36 **Which then of the bounties of your Lord will you deny?**

Within the boundaries of the heavens and earth a point comes when the penetrations cease. There is a limit to every system and every creational situation. *Jinn* and *ins* can penetrate into the heavens, as man has done in the last few decades. But there will be zones in the heavens through which man will not be able to pass because of the great activity of meteorites or because of the presence of radiation or some other factors. As there are limits established in man's outward travel, so are there limits to which he may travel inwardly. The Prophet, *salla-llãhu 'alayhi wa ãlihi wa sallam*, said: "I was not given of inner knowledge but little." These are the laws of Reality. How can man deny the mercies of Allah? Even the limitations and their meanings—the fact that man is imprisoned in time and space—are great bounties.

فَإِذَا انشَقَّتِ السَّمَآءُ فَكَانَتْ وَرْدَةً كَالدِّهَانِ

37 **So when the heaven is rent asunder, and then becomes red like hide,**

فَبِأَيِّ اٰلَآءِ رَبِّكُمَا تُكَذِّبٰنِ

38 **Which then of the bounties of your Lord will you deny?**

The time will come when the heavens—which are impenetrable, limited, and built as though firm—will break apart. *Shaqqa* (شقّ) means to split. As creation is fragmented, another state will take hold of it, one in which heat dominates. At present, the heat of the planets and stars is in equilibrium. In our planetary system, an example of disequilibrium is found in the form of sunspots. Whenever they occur on the sun there are disturbances in the planetary system, though none are great enough to throw it out of balance. The system of counterbalanced forces will break when this journey in the cosmos reaches its point of maturity.

The same shattering occurs to man. While he lives, his spiritual and physical bodies hold together. Man contains an echo or an image of the entire cosmos. All of the functions in man's body are in equilibrium---his faculties, all of the electrical charges that run through his brain, the miles of nerves. This amazing entity will fall apart when the soul leaves. It then immediately will start to decay. That is what will happen to the heavens: the laws that hold them together will break and they will just disintegrate.

فَيَوْمَئِذٍ لَّا يُسْئَلُ عَن ذَنبِهِ إِنسٌ وَلَا جَآنٌّ

39 **So on that day neither man nor jinn shall be asked about his sin.**

فَبِأَىِّ الَآءِ رَبِّكُمَا تُكَذِّبَنِ

40 **Which then of the bounties of your Lord will you deny?**

While the previous group of *ãyat* spoke of the outer heavens, this group speaks of the inner space of the individual. Every *rûh* will spontaneously transmit what it has gathered in the tuning period of life in this world. There will be nothing to ask, because the question will already have been answered.

Man in this life may be in *nifãq* (نفاق ,hypocrisy). He may hide his fears, anxieties and suspicions. *Nafaq* (نفق), related to *nifãq,* means a tunnel. Man enters one hole to come out from another. He is forever tunneling, trying to escape. The end to his efforts to escape comes when questioning ceases and he becomes an 'answer'. Then he will beam and transmit the state in which he had left this world. If he has been transmitting the Qur'ãn, then he will be close to the main transmitter, Allah; he will be one of the *ashabu-l-yamîn* (اصحاب اليمين ,the companions of the right). If he has been transmitting his own song which has his desires, expectations and self-righteousness mixed into it, then his transmission will be as good as that mixture.

يُعْرَفُ الْمُجْرِمُونَ بِسِيمٰهُمْ فَيُؤْخَذُ بِالنَّوَاصِي وَالْاَقْدَامِ

41 **The guilty will be recognized by their marks, so they will be seized by the forelocks and the feet.**

فَبِاَيِّ اٰلَاۤءِ رَبِّكُمَا تُكَذِّبٰنِ

42 **Which then of the bounties of your Lord will you deny?**

Everyone is caught by what he has put forth in his movements and his actions. Those who have not let their hearts be *qulûb* (plural of *qalb*), have committed crimes against themselves. They will not have seen the *husn* (حسن , perfection) in this world nor will they have known tawhîd. Those who have been deprived of tawhîd and the knowledge of the One are known *bisîmahum* (بسيما هم), by their face, their marks, their scars. Those who have allowed their hearts to be turned have set their hearts free. Only then can man see the truth of every situation. In the next life, however, there is an immediate recognition. Here one recognizes the outer folds of the face, the wrinkles, or the coloration, but there one sees Oneness because there is no longer any duality: there is only One.

Nawãsî (نواصى) are foreheads. The forehead of the upright human projects out. It is as though man wants to connect to something in front of him. Allah says that man is caught by his highest point, which is his forehead, and his lowest, which is his feet. There is no escape for him now, so how can he still deny the Truth? He is the outcome of what he has put forth, of where his feet have taken him and to what his forehead has made *sajda*.

هٰذِهٖ جَهَنَّمُ الَّتِىْ يُكَذِّبُ بِهَا الْمُجْرِمُوْنَ

43 **This is the hell which the guilty call a lie.**

يَطُوْفُوْنَ بَيْنَهَا وَبَيْنَ حَمِيْمٍ اٰنٍ

44 **Round about they will go, between it and hot, boiling water.**

فَبِاَىِّ اٰلَاۤءِ رَبِّكُمَا تُكَذِّبٰنِ

45 **Which then of the bounties of your Lord will you deny?**

Jahannam (جهنم) is the final abode of those who are in the fire. It is *jahnîm* (جهنيم), the bottomless pit. Those who are in the fire have tasted a bit of it in this life but denied its reality. Everyone in this life has tasted it. If man had not tasted it, it would be meaningless to him. Sayyidna Adam, *'alayhi-s-salãm*, had not experienced a lie, so when *shaytãn* told him to taste the fruit, to wish for something else, to be discontent, he did not know better and believed him. But this is not the case with us. We have tasted the fire and the garden. If we did not know these things there would be incongruity in the balance. Everyone knows the meaning of uncertainty, disturbance, agitation, fear, anxiety, hatred and anger---all of these are fire. If man leaves them in himself long enough, they can create a stomach ulcer, which is an internal fire. It has been found that having a burning stomach is far more disturbing than having burnt skin, because it is internal, and therefore more potent. The fire is the lot of the criminal who has committed crimes against himself and yet denies them

Yatûfûna is from *tãfa* (طاف), to walk about, to wander around. *Tawwãf* (طوّاف) is derived from it and means going around in circles, circumambulating. The inhabitants of the fire move from burning hot to boiling water.

Tawf (طوف) is a wall encompassing a garden. A word which echoes *tãfa*, that is, which has a different root while sounding very similar, is *tayf* (طيف), which means shadow, dream or fantasy. In the Arabic language, certain words sound very similar to others, a phenomenon which evokes a subliminal association in meaning. If one hears tawwãf one might, quite naturally, recall *tawf* and *tayf*, though they are known to have specifically different meanings. It is like going into a multi-screen circular theater which screens many films simultaneously: you are forced to glance at the screens closest to the film you are viewing.

The root system of the Arabic language is a vast receptacle of meanings. All the words of a similar sound have the potential to lead one to a single root, as the example of *tawf* and *tayf* illustrates. In life, man goes around and around without stopping, as if hallucinating, but when he comes to the *tawf* (wall) he stops. Most of the Arabic words that sound similar but have different roots have a semantic relationship.

Those who are at a loss in this world have denied the Rahmãn in the next world. They are in the same situation in both worlds. They move from the frying pan into the fire. Man moves from one job to another that is even worse. He leaves one wife and enters into an even worse relationship. He does not realize it is Allah's love hitting him, urging him to stop. This life is but a short prelude to the next life.

وَلِمَنْ خَافَ مَقَامَ رَبِّهِ جَنَّتٰنِ

46 **And for he who fears standing before his Lord are two gardens.**

فَبِاَيِّ اٰلَاۤءِ رَبِّكُمَا تُكَذِّبٰنِ

47 **Which then of the bounties of your Lord will you deny?**

ذَوَاتَآ اَفْنَانٍ

48 **Having in them various kinds.**

فَبِاَيِّ اٰلَاۤءِ رَبِّكُمَا تُكَذِّبٰنِ

49 **Which then of the bounties of your Lord will you deny?**

"And for he who fears standing before his Lord," who recognized the Lordship, who recognized that there is One entity in charge, who feared transgressing His laws and was completely in His hands, for him there are two gardens. One of them is the garden of *arwãh* (ارواح), the garden of the spirits—it is the garden of eternal bliss. The other is the garden of hearts, the garden of *mushãhada* (مشاهدة), eternal witnessing. These are two inner gardens. There are many other examples of pairs of gardens: the garden of experiencing and the garden of recognition; the garden of wakefulness and the garden of sleep; the garden of the *mashriq* (مشرق ,east) and the garden of the *maghrib* (مغرب , west); the gardens of the beginning and of the end.

فِيهِمَا عَيْنَٰنِ تَجْرِيَانِ

50 **In both of them are two fountains flowing.**

فَبِأَيِّ الَآءِ رَبِّكُمَا تُكَذِّبَانِ

51 **Which then of the bounties of your Lord will you deny?**

In the garden, there are two fountains and there are two springs that flow. They are nourished in an invisible way, just as man's heart is also nourished. Man does not know how love is fed. When people gather together to bury someone who was loved by them, how is it that the dead may revive the love in living hearts? It is a hidden spring, a hidden river. It reminds people of Allah, the Taker and the Giver of life. Death reminds man of his end so that he becomes less fossilized, arrogant and hard-hearted.

فِيهِمَا مِنْ كُلِّ فَاكِهَةٍ زَوْجَانِ

52 **In both of them are pairs of every fruit.**

فَبِأَيِّ الَآءِ رَبِّكُمَا تُكَذِّبَانِ

53 **Which then of the bounties of your Lord will you deny?**

مُتَّكِئِينَ عَلَى فُرُشٍ بَطَآئِنُهَا مِنْ إِسْتَبْرَقٍ ط وَجَنَا الْجَنَّتَيْنِ دَانٍ

54 **Reclining on beds, the inner coverings of which are of silk brocade; and the fruits of the two gardens are within reach.**

فَبِاَيِّ اٰلَاۤءِ رَبِّكُمَا تُكَذِّبٰنِ

55 **Which then of the bounties of your Lord will you deny?**

How can man deny the bounties of Allah? In the gardens there are fruits of every kind, fruits which make you *fakih* (فكه , gay,cheerful). In the gardens there are two different flowing rivers of bounty: man and woman.

Muttaki'îna (متكئين ,reclining, plural of *muttaki*) implies that there is available all that could be imagined in the way of comfort, luxury and relaxation. It implies being in a state of great tranquility, your heart at rest. This is, of course, never possible in this life, because as soon as one becomes comfortable, an annoyance occurs that must be dealt with. Dealing with it causes another sort of reaction, and so on. The agitation in this life is never ending.

فِيهِنَّ قٰصِرٰتُ الطَّرْفِ لَمْ يَطْمِثْهُنَّ اِنْسٌ قَبْلَهُمْ وَلَا جَآنٌّ

56 **In them are those who restrain themselves; man nor jinn have not touched them before.**

فَبِاَيِّ اٰلَاۤءِ رَبِّكُمَا تُكَذِّبٰنِ

57 **Which then of the bounties of your Lord will you deny?**

كَاَنَّهُنَّ الْيَاقُوتُ وَ الْمَرْجَانُ

58 **As though they were rubies and coral.**

فَبِاَيِّ اٰلَآءِ رَبِّكُمَا تُكَذِّبٰنِ

59 **Which then of the bounties of your Lord will you deny?**

Qãsirãtu-t-tarf (قاصرات الطرف) are those who restrain themselves, who lower their gaze. *Qãsirãt* is in the feminine gender and implies that they are man's opposite. Man and his opposite are like the positive and the negative which, when put together, make one by neutralization. These women are not desirous but are available to bring about contentment. They have never been touched and are ever pure. Their virginal state stops man from imagining the physical vulgarity to which he is accustomed in this world. This implies purity of a higher state. This state is based on a timeless equilibrium. The instant there is a desire, it is made quiet.

There is never any real satisfaction in any relationship in this life except for the relationship between the slave and his Master. In every other relationship in this world there is blame. A man blames his wife and she blames him, while nobody blames himself—and so it never ends. People end up having had five wives and five divorces. Man expects the highest from others while not having expected the highest of himself. A person who can live with one partner can live with any wife. If he can live with himself, he can live with anyone else. Man blames others, claiming that they are wrong: they do not lower their eyes nor do they have the right courtesy.

"As though they were rubies and coral." Rubies and coral scintillate in their purity. The ultimate beauty of nature is pure and simple, without interference or compromise. In the garden women have not had to beautify themselves. They too are real and pure.

هَلْ جَزَآءُ الْإِحْسَانِ إِلَّا الْإِحْسَانُ

60 **Is the reward of goodness but goodness?**

فَبِأَيِّ آلَآءِ رَبِّكُمَا تُكَذِّبَانِ

61 **Which then of the bounties of your Lord will you deny?**

Is not the reward of good action, good action itself? Every action has its equal and opposite reaction. If you have done good it will come back to you. But is that goodness done for Allah, or is it for your own whims? Many people think they are acting correctly, while in reality they are at a loss. There is a *hadîth*, a tradition, which says: "The sleep of the '*ãlim* (عالم ,one who knows), is better than the wakefulness of the worshipper." Wakefulness is measured by the degree of knowledge and recognition of the worshipped.

Many people are striving for right action, establishing orphanages and so on. If they expect those whom they help to fall at their feet in gratitude, it means these so-called generous people are not serving for Allah's sake. "Is the reward of goodness but goodness?" is often used incorrectly. If one's action is honorable, it will only have a like reaction. Is the *ihsãn*(احسان, the best action) not for He Who created man, Who gave man the possibility of unending realities? The service that man renders for the *Rahmãn* should be the best. How else can man repay the *Rahmãn*? How can he repay the mercy of Allah other than by reflecting His attributes? Could the Prophet of Allah, salla-llãhu *'alayhi wa ãlihi wa sallam*, be other than the greatest of creation and the mercy of Allah upon the worlds? The faithfulness of the slave to his Lord is exemplified by all the prophets in their actions, and the best we can do is to follow in the dust of their footsteps.

وَمِن دُونِهِمَا جَنَّتَانِ

62 **And besides these two are two (other) gardens.**

فَبِأَيِّ آلَاءِ رَبِّكُمَا تُكَذِّبَانِ

63 **Which then of the bounties of your Lord will you deny?**

مُدْهَامَّتَانِ

64 **Both inclining to blackness.**

فَبِأَيِّ آلَاءِ رَبِّكُمَا تُكَذِّبَانِ

65 **Which then of the bounties of your Lord will you deny?**

فِيهِمَا عَيْنَانِ نَضَّاخَتَانِ

66 **In both of them are two springs gushing forth.**

فَبِأَيِّ آلَاءِ رَبِّكُمَا تُكَذِّبَانِ

67 **Which then of the bounties of your Lord will you deny?**

فِيهِمَا فَاكِهَةٌ وَنَخْلٌ وَرُمَّانٌ

68 **In both are fruits and palms and pomegranates.**

فَبِأَيِّ الَاءِ رَبِّكُمَا تُكَذِّبٰنِ

69 **Which then of the bounties of your Lord will you deny?**

Besides the two gardens are two others, the gardens of those who fear to stand before Allah in the next life: "Both inclining to blackness." *Mudhãmmatãn* (مدهامتان), related to the root *idhamma*, means that which is of a dark green color inclining to black, as gardens from being much watered. Still these gardens are not of the pure light which is the essence of everything.

In both of these gardens are two springs. Within every event one finds two situations, within each duality there is yet another duality—in the sensory and in the meaning. The unfoldment of duality within duality is unending. If one reflects upon this world and its affairs, one will find that there is no end to that reflection. Reflection is a sea whose shores end up with Reality, with knowledge. Within Reality there is an immense sea: the more one looks into it the more one finds two.

فِيهِنَّ خَيْرٰتٌ حِسَانٌ

70 **In them are goodly things, beautiful ones.**

فَبِأَيِّ الَاءِ رَبِّكُمَا تُكَذِّبٰنِ

71 **Which then of the bounties of your Lord will you deny?**

In the garden there are beautiful ones from whom comes only *khayr* (خير , good). In man's state on earth there cannot be *khayr* without bad enveloping it. Every good action that man wants to initiate is surrounded by the possibilities of wrong action. He has to wade and cut through the jungle of wrong action to get to right action. The way of *shaytãn* is easy, but the way of right action is difficult. Allah says that only *khayr* comes from these beauties.

In the beauty of this world lies its opposite, ugliness. Whatever anything may be, think of it when it is decaying and stinking. Think of a pond of beautiful water lilies, then think of them in winter and how they die and rot. Think of a beautiful young woman, then think of her when she is old and decrepit. Beauty in this realm contains within it ugliness, whereas in the next realm there is only beauty within the *khayrãtun hisãn* (خيرات حسان , goodly things, beautiful ones).

حُورٌ مَّقۡصُورَٰتٌ فِى ٱلۡخِيَامِ

72 **Pure ones confined to the pavilions.**

فَبِأَىِّ ءَالَآءِ رَبِّكُمَا تُكَذِّبَانِ

73 **Which then of the bounties of your Lord will you deny?**

Hûr (حور ,virgins of paradise) are in the highest state of courtesy and purity, which is actually what man desires. The pure ones are confined to pavilions, ready and waiting to neutralize any duality that might be introduced by man's arrival. *Khiyãm* (خيام) are tents, enclosures which stabilize what has been unfulfilled.

لَمْ يَطْمِثْهُنَّ اِنْسٌ قَبْلَهُمْ وَلَا جَآنٌّ

74 **Man has not touched them before nor jinn.**

فَبِاَيِّ اٰلَآءِ رَبِّكُمَا تُكَذِّبٰنِ

75 **Which then of the bounties of your Lord will you deny?**

The *hûr* have never been touched, existing as if 'charged.' Once a charged object has been touched it no longer retains its charge. They are pure powers, not women with legs and hands. Coming into the next life men become neutralized by contact with them and become unified.

مُتَّكِئِيْنَ عَلٰى رَفْرَفٍ خُضْرٍ وَّعَبْقَرِيٍّ حِسَانٍ

76 **Reclining on green cushions and beautiful carpets.**

فَبِاَيِّ اٰلَآءِ رَبِّكُمَا تُكَذِّبٰنِ

77 **Which then of the bounties of your Lord will you deny?**

'Abqarî (عبقرى) is a colorful carpet and can also mean a genius. *'Abqar* is a legendary place inhabited by jinn. It is the name of certain comforts and joys that men get in this world, that state of reclining which the people of the garden attain. No longer confined by their bodies, they are pure awareness.

تبٰرَكَ اسْمُ رَبِّكَ ذِى الْجَلٰلِ وَالْاِكْرَامِ

78 **Blessed be the name of your Lord, the Lord of Glory and Honor!**

This *sûra* begins with an ãya which is a proof, a sign and a manifestation. The first is the *Rahmãn*, Who taught the knowledge of Himself through the Mîzãn, the Qur'ãn. Allah's first manifestation was his light, the light of knowledge. The *kãfirun* (كافرون ,deniers) desire to put out the light of Allah and His order, but Allah does not allow it because "Allah is the light of the heavens and earth."

The *sûra* ends with *tabãraka* (تبارک , blessed be). Blessed is the name of Allah. If man calls Allah's name, Allah approaches his dwelling.

Man, in this life, is on a journey. He has in his hand a ticket, which instead of reading 'Chicago', reads 'Allah'. Allah is the ticket and the port is the *nafs.* If man goes through that port, if he passes his *nafs*, then he is on his way towards that Name. When he reaches the Name It is one with Reality. While travelling, the traveler might say that he is going to Chicago, but the ticket itself is not the experience of Chicago. The experience of the place does not begin until he is actually there.

Man is as good as his intention. Stop time—press time together rather than telescoping it as is done in the life-experience—and the name and its reality become one. If man's heart is completely in Chicago then the name will be unified with its reality. If man's ticket is in his hand, if he has recognized the *baraka* of the *Rahmãn*, then he has taken the Name as a key, then he has reached the goal. The door will come to the key. He will find the *Rabb* (رب , Lord) already there. The Lord has nothing other than the highest love for this creation, which contains every meaning—which is man.

Lordship has in it all the honor and the glory. In this impossible situation of the world, man strives to be glorified and honored but finds it futile because the honor and glory belong to Allah. If man honors and glorifies Him, he comes to see only Him. Then the opinions of others, whether good or bad, mean nothing to him. People admire him, he does not mind. They curse him, he does not mind, because, having put himself in the lowest possible position, his mind is on Allah. Allah's reaction to his behavior is the opposite: He bestows upon him real honor, not human honor.

The door and key to the knowledge of the *Rahmãn*, the knowledge of the all-encompassing Beneficent, is the recognition of His *baraka*, the recognition of His blessedness. Whichever way man turns he sees blessedness. If his experience is sweet it is blessedness, if it is bitter it is blessedness. If there is peace it is blessedness, if there is war it is blessedness. How can there be peace without war? How can there be health without an illness? How can there be Islam without a boundary beyond which are its enemies? There is *dãru-l-Islãm* (دار السلام , house of Islam) and *dãru-l-kufr* (دار الكفر , house of denial); there cannot be one without the other. How can life be treasured and valued maximally unless there is death? How can there be awareness unless there is numbness, as experienced in this life as wakefulness and sleep? Both states are glorious and a blessing from Allah.

How can there be *nafs* in man and yet no *nafs* in him? The knowledge of the *nafs*, once it is experienced, is one of the highest blessings, because it is the knowledge of the *Rabb*. If man is faithful, if he has trust, then he will continuously see the *rahma* of the *Rahmãn* in every aspect. That is the positive contentment of the Muslim. He has discrimination, the ability to discern a healthy atmosphere from an unhealthy one; but within both he recognizes the blessedness. His contented heart guides him to the right and correct action, to *ihsãn*. What is the maqãmu-l-ihsãn, the station of excellence, but acting as though

Allah sees you, even though you do not see Allah? Man must attain purer action until he is, as an individual, doing his *wus'* (وسع), his utmost according to his ability. Then he is in the right place, at the right time, doing the right thing. That is the garden. The reward of *ihsãn* is *ihsãn*.

If a man can do something better than what he is doing now, he should do it. He should be completely fulfilled. Once that point has been reached, he will have burst out of his self-imposed constraints. He would not be where he does not belong, he would not be where he does not get the maximum benefit, because he recognizes every breath. Imãm 'Ali, *'alayhi-s-salãm*, said, "What is *halal* (حلال , lawful) for you is counted and what is *harãm* (حرام, forbidden) for you is punished." Because breath, being a gift of the *Rahmãn*, is *halãl* upon man, he must account for how he uses it.

The reward of high action is a high reward. The highest of rewards is the recognition of the honor and the glory of the Lord to Whom man is enslaved. If he is a totally pure and faithful slave, then His glory and His honor will also be upon him. The true slave is a servant. You will find that if someone in a corporation is an efficient personal assistant for the chairman, he is more feared and respected in that firm than anybody else, because it is known that he is well tuned to his master. If the slave is truly an abandoned slave, he reflects the glory, the majesty and the honor of the *Rahmãn*.

(٥٦) سورة الواقعة مكية
وآياتها ست وتسعون

SURAT UL-WAQI'A

THE EVENT

Introduction

This Makkan *sûra* describes the major resurrection when all is brought forth and appropriate segregation and perfect justice take place.

The *sûra* presents existential evidence to enable man to question the reason for his existence, and for him to uplift himself to the realization of the one Creator, Who is the only One deserving of adoration and worship.

بِسْمِ اللَّهِ الرَّحْمَٰنِ الرَّحِيمِ

In the name of Allah, the Beneficent, the Merciful.

Everything is by the name of Allah. The *bismi-llah* (بسم الله,in the name of Allah) is part of every *sûra* except one, at-*Tawba. Bismi-llahi-r-Rahmani-Rahim* has a literal meaning that is always the same, but its message differs according to the meaning of the sûra with which it is connected. Those who believe, and whose belief has been confirmed by varying degrees of personal awakening and experience, see the one hand behind everything which is manifest, as well as that which is not manifest. They see the subtle behind the gross. Everything has the label of Reality on it. Whatever you do or do not cognize, every attribute or action, is marked by its cause.

The *bismi-llah* is the gate which, if opened properly, will lead you into the garden of its *sûra*. It is a determined part of each *sûra* and as such should be read in the prayer as belonging to it. In the prayer one should choose the *sûra* first, then say the *bismi-llah* in the name of He who has given you the power of declaring *tawhîd* (توحيد , divine unity), allowing it to flow into the *sûra* as one thought.

إِذَا وَقَعَتِ الْوَاقِعَةُ

1 **When the great event comes to pass,**

لَيْسَ لِوَقْعَتِهَا كَاذِبَةٌ

2 **There is no belying its coming to pass**

خَافِضَةٌ رَّافِعَةٌ

3 **Abasing (one party), exalting (the other),**

"When the great event comes to pass." *Waqa'a* (وقع) means to fall, to befall, to happen. The event which concerns man is the promised event of the Resurrection, the *yawm ul-qiyama* (يوم القيامة), the day of the beginning of the next phase of man's experience. It is the main point of reference and of the greatest importance. Whatever exists in the next cycle of creation—not being based on the duality in which there is confusion of body and soul—is not subject to time. Whatever exists or can be experienced from the moment of the great event onward, has its reflection in this life. For example, in the Qur'ãn, the fire that is promised in the next life is referred to as *nar ul-jahannam* (نار الجهنّم , the fire of hell) or *nar ul-kubra* (نار الكبرى , the great fire), implying that what you experience in this life is the small fire in the form of anger, disappointment, agitation and unfulfilled desires. Also the experience of the garden is potentially with man here and now. In the same way, the experience of the event, the day of reckoning, can be echoed and reflected within man here and now.

When a significant event occurs in someone's life it can cause him to begin to witness or to fully awaken. Such an event brings light into the passage of existence. Man is moving in a tunnel propelled by the powers of nature, guided or misguided by habits of the past, circumstances of the present and projections of the future. He is in a cocoon. If there is a sudden break in it and that crack begins to widen, then for the person who has experienced it there is a major event, there is a *waqi'a* (واقعه). But when the great event, the *yawm ul-qiyam*a, occurs, nobody can deny it. Everyone is subject to its power. It lifts up and brings down, blowing up planets, stars or aspects of the cosmos and collapsing other parts. One creation ends and another begins. The cosmic entities are compelled to move in opposite directions. A major uplifting, down-thrusting situation will occur.

It is the time when the hearts that are already enlightened are lifted and stripped of their burdens, and the hearts that have been tarnished and burdened are brought down. The *mu'min* (مؤمن , believer) is elevated and the *kafir* (كافر ,denier) or *munafiq* (منافق , hypocrite) is degraded. The day of reckoning is the final sorting out, the *yawm ul-fasl* (يوم الفصل , the day of separation into groups). There are no gray areas; your state will be joy or misery, according to what you have directed yourself toward and earned during the short preface of this life. Those who have been uplifting themselves along the path of truth will be fully uplifted in the next life, and those who have been degrading themselves will be completely degraded. The next consciousness is timeless, and will therefore have the stamp of permanency upon it. That is why it is called the final abode, for in it there is no movement.

إِذَا رُجَّتِ الْأَرْضُ رَجًّا

4 **When the earth shall be shaken with a (severe) shaking,**

وَبُسَّتِ الْجِبَالُ بَسًّا

5 **And the mountains shall be made to crumble with (an awful) crumbling,**

فَكَانَتْ هَبَآءً مُّنبَثًّا

6 **So that they shall be as scattered dust,**

"When the earth shall be shaken with a (severe) shaking." *Ard* (ارض , earth) is whatever serves as a foundation, such as land. *Rajja* (رجّ) is to shake. Everyone wants stability, whether in one's home, relationships, or in the economy. But those who seek absolute stability find that it only exists when there is trust in Allah. Every other stability is relative. Even though it may last his lifetime, the seeker knows that the world and the cosmos are on a journey, and that the foundation upon which he has built his relative security may get shaken and pulled out from under him. At the time of the shaking, the flimsy relative foundation, having served its purpose in this creational cycle, is finished. For the man on the path such a calamity is regarded as direct evidence of the love of Reality for him. He therefore looks for some better foundation until he discovers the foundation of all foundations.

The solid mass, which came to equilibrium after the earth cooled down, giving it relative stability, will crumble into dust. The fortunate one who has intellect comes to realize that what he perceives as the solidity of his foundation is only in his mind. Nothing in this world is going to last, whether it be health, wealth or children. Once that is recognized, the awareness, immediacy and urgency of the quest become the major preoccupation in his life, and all other aspects become secondary and therefore acceptable because of their transiency. After his foundation has been shaken and destroyed, a new and much firmer foundation is built.

The measurement of worldly things is based upon specific time factors which are very different if there is a turning of the heart, resulting from a turning over of one's situation. It is a matter of attitude. The dislodging of the heart from this world is truly and genuinely a major event. It is a prelude to the experience of after-life. The heart is then totally uprooted and enters a state beyond freedom, for freedom is only meaningful because there are shackles. Man is capable of grasping this state intellectually and experientially, to varying degrees of clarity. For example, the most solid visible realities in this existence are the mountains which anchor the mantle of the earth. If these entities which are considered most solid can be torn free, then consider those things which are as flimsy as one's relationships or thoughts.

"They shall be as scattered dust." When the final event occurs there are definite streams into which everyone is segregated. In this world the streams are not clearly delineated because we perceive things in relative degrees, and that relativity blurs the delineations.

وَّكُنتُمْ أَزْوَاجًا ثَلَٰثَةً

7 **And you shall be three sorts.**

فَأَصْحَٰبُ الْمَيْمَنَةِ ۙ مَآ أَصْحَٰبُ الْمَيْمَنَةِ

8 **Then (as to) the companions of the right hand; how happy are the companions of the right hand!**

Man is sorted out into three types. At the final event there is a filtering process that takes place in much the same way as it occurs in this life. In one group there are those who are in *îmãn* (ايمان , faith, trust), whose trust originates either from intellectual reasoning or through its inheritance from a family that believes in Reality, in Islam. In another are those who are at a loss, who are confused and arrogant. They are the people whose egos are so solid that they totally deny Reality. But these types are not always bound to their groups. There are occasions in which individuals leave the stream of those in loss and confusion to join the stream of those in utter trust, unshakable trust, which is based upon the knowledge of the one and only Reality.

The people of the right are the true people of *îmãn*. They believe in Allah and in His divine mercy upon His creation. They believe that the purpose of creation is to recognize the Creator and abandon their will into the will of the Creator, *îmãn* begins by outer submission, and ends with the direct recognition that one's will and what is decreed by Allah are one: they emanated from the One, are sustained by the One and will return to the One. At this stage man realizes the source of inner joy, for there is no longer any resistance.

The people of the right hand have acted positively and directly. The right hand in the Arabic culture, as well as in many other cultures, is the hand of willful and knowledgeable transaction, while the left hand is the hand of giving up and throwing away, the hand of negation.

وَأَصْحَٰبُ ٱلْمَشْـَٔمَةِ مَآ أَصْحَٰبُ ٱلْمَشْـَٔمَةِ

9 **And (as to) the companions of the left hand; how wretched are the companions of the left hand!**

Mash'ama (مشامة ,the left hand) is from *sha'ama* (شأم), and means to perceive a bad omen, to foretell a calamity or to be unlucky. The people of the left are left-overs, having cursed themselves by their ignorance and loss. Man cannot question the Creator; he is given a description of Reality, a reference to the *yawm ul-qiyama* with which he may not interfere. In his life he may feel that he is at a loss, angry, unhappy and confused, yet he must realize that there is still the possibility of an awakening that may take him to the people of the right and he must continue striving.

وَالسّٰبِقُوْنَ السّٰبِقُوْنَ

10 **And the foremost are the foremost,**

اُولٰئِكَ الْمُقَرَّبُوْنَ

11 **These are they who are drawn near (to Allah),**

"And the foremost are the foremost." *Sabaqa* (سبق) is to be ahead, to precede. In this life everyone is either leading or being led. Allah refers here to the state of ultimate success which is the success of the one who has moved into the zone of the beyond time, the next creation. According to some traditions, the *sabiqun* (السابقون) were those who early on were in *îmãn*. The Îmãns identify some of the early *mu'minun* who went to the garden as the son of Adam who was murdered, the first man who embraced Islam from among Pharoah's people, *Habib an-Najar* who followed Sayyidna 'Isa, *'alayhi-s-salãm*, and *'Ali ibn Abi Talib, 'alayhi-s-salãm*.

As-sabiqun (السابقون) generally refers to those who will be in the garden without question, being already in that state in this life. They are the near ones, the ones who have come first. Traditionally, the people of *tafsir* (تفسير , Qur'ãnic commentary) have said that it refers to all the Prophets. The Prophet himself, *salla-llãhu 'alayhi wa ãlihi wa sallam*, said: "It refers to those who are close to my way." Those who have fully taken on the Muhammadi path have no account to render because they were rendering their account at all times during their lives. They had already been in a complete state of abandonment.

فِى جَنّٰتِ النَّعِيمِ

12 **In the gardens of bliss.**

ثُلَّةٌ مِّنَ الْاَوَّلِينَ

13 **A numerous company from among the first,**

وَقَلِيلٌ مِّنَ الْاٰخِرِينَ

14 **And a few from among the latter.**

They are "in the gardens of bliss." *Na'im* (نعيم) is from *na'ama* (نعم), to live in comfort, ease. *Ni'ma* (نعمة) is a blessing, anything one wants to have more of. "It may be that you dislike a thing while it is good for you." (*al-Baqara*: 216). Often something comes to man in which he does not see the goodness. If man were to see what befalls him as being in the name of Allah, the Beneficent, the Merciful, *bismi-llahi-r-Rahmani-r-Rahim*, then he would see the mercy behind every event and every situation. Otherwise he would be judging from his individual point of view. The *mu'min* only sees goodness no matter how it may look to others. If he is in true *îmãn*, if he believes that the controller of this creation is the *Rahman*, he will try to see the *rahma* of Allah behind every event. For that reason, the *mu'min's* heart is never baffled, shocked, or disturbed. The *mu'min* acts as best he can because he is both actor and acted upon. Outwardly, he will respond to an emergency, while inwardly, he will be content, knowing that it came from the Reality. If he dislikes what happens to him it is because he has judged it incorrectly and erroneously.

Judgement is based on the degree of ignorance and knowledge. "And it may be that you love a thing while it is evil for you." (*al-Baqara*:216) A child loves to be buried under a mound of chocolate, whereas a grownup with knowledge may recognize the damage it can cause his health. A responsible young man does not realize the affliction and the responsibility that comes with wealth until he earns it by the sweat of his brow; then he recognizes the difficulty of acquiring it, keeping it and dispensing it correctly. An irresponsible person, however, has a romantic desire for things without knowing what danger and affliction accompany them.

A group of those who came earlier to the knowledge of Reality came earlier to the garden of *îmãn*. They were early in the sense that they arrived at the garden before death, having achieved in this life the state of joy, tranquility and abandonment. They already knew the meaning of bliss and had a direct knowledge of *tawhîd* in this world. Those who have not obtained direct knowledge can only improve their prayers and supplications in the hope that they will get it when this chain of the body and the world is removed by death. No matter how much one is in *tawhîd* and *îmãn*]there is still the pull of the body. It is another of Allah's reminders that one is held by the chain of this realm of existence. It does not matter to what extent one is in total abandonment, duality and loss are still recognized.

Human injustice exists because the ultimate height in spiritual evolution, which is the historical or worldly event of the appearance of the *Mahdi* (مهدى , literally the rightly guided one; he is the twelfth Îmãn who is in concealment), has not occurred. At that time, the earth will be inherited by the humble people of right action and Allah's justice will be fully manifest in this life.

If one is concerned about time, then one is concerned about the chronology of events. If the light of intellect enables one to go beyond time for just a moment, then "early" implies those who simply got the message, regardless of when. Those whose main concern is to live the life of *tawhîd* are inclined to place less importance upon time. The man who seeks unification seeks to obtain Sayyidna Ibrahim's knowledge, he seeks the company of the Prophet, *salla-llãhu 'alayhi wa ãlihi wa sallam*, and desires the guidance, counsel and companionship of the Îmãns and the select *sahaba* (صحا بة ,companions). He wishes to be close to their state. It is meaningless to desire closeness to them physically, without desiring to take of what they possess of meanings. And if one wishes closeness to their state it can occur at any time, because their states are expounded to man through the Qur'ãn, the *sunna* (سنة ,Prophetic custom) and *Hadith* (حديث, tradition). One is living in their presence if one has access to the gate of their state.

عَلَىٰ سُرُرٍ مَّوْضُونَةٍ

15 **On thrones decorated,**

مُّتَّكِئِينَ عَلَيْهَا مُتَقَٰبِلِينَ

16 **Reclining on them, facing one another.**

The root of *surûr* (سرر ,thrones) is *sarra* (سرّ), which is to make happy, to confide a secret, to hide something. From it come many words that form an interesting pattern of meanings. *Surûr* (سرور) is joy, implying that the source of joy is a secret that can only be whispered to oneself. It is the secret of secrets and cannot be divulged. If one is happy, happiness is itself the explanation of that state, but one cannot give the source of that state to someone else. It relates to another level of consciousness.

A pleasure is something one can share, something one can buy. It is related to attachments and is a worldly thing while *surûr*, joy, is for its own sake. The bird sings because its nature is to sing, irrespective of whether the hunter is hunting it or the neighborhood is giving it extra food. A pleasure is the result of something that has occurred. A person is lonely, then he meets a companion who echoes much of what he believes in—that is a pleasure. Someone was hungry, there was emptiness in his stomach and it was filled by food—that is a pleasure. Pleasure is like neutralization: the negative and the positive meet and are neutralized.

Joy is something else; it is the negation of the negative. Joy occurs when what was considered to be desirable has been recognized as being *wahm* (وهم), illusion. Negation of the negative is positive and that is the normal state of man. It is for this reason that man inherently seeks joy. He knows pleasure, he knows it is purchasable, but he does not readily know the way to joy. Man seeks happiness because it is his real nature. He is unhappy because he has been telling himself that he needs a certain something to be happy. He constantly runs after it, but as soon as he gets it, he desires something else.

The door to the abode of joy is the recognition of how to unknot what one has knotted. That is why it is said that the source is a secret within a secret. A desirable thing is in itself a *wahm*. The recognition of the *wahm* is the negation of it. And if that negation is genuine, then the root of joy is being nourished from within. That is the soil in which the tree of contentment will grow. Contentment is a tree that nobody can transplant into anybody else. One has to, through one's own labor, nurture it and make it grow.

There is inherent contentment in a created being such as a bird, but man has the consciousness of contentment. Furthermore, he has the light of consciousness of consciousness. This establishes man as the highest of creation. Man is conscious of the consciousness of happiness. He is conscious of the consciousness of unhappiness.

surûr cannot be passed on, it has to be earned. If one has grasped the way to its attainment one will constantly seek after it in one's life. It has nothing to do with time or place. Often, an ignorant man returns to the lake or the mountain top where he had spent a holiday or had had a good time, thinking that he can reproduce the inner state of a momentary opening of the heart. He yearns for the upliftment of joyfulness. This perverted seeking is found among the inspired souls of people such as artists and composers. In the biographies of these madmen, one will find that they often go back to the same mountain spot or shack, to live for the rest of their lives in a romantic illusion so that they can reproduce their creative moments. But creative moments are moments of detachment from this world. It simply happened that he was there in that chalet on that mountain top. He yearns for the moment of joy he experienced but cannot retrieve it. He thinks joy is prescribable or describable but it is not. "The path of those upon whom Thou hast bestowed favors. Not (the path) of those upon whom Thy wrath is brought down, nor of those who go astray." (*al-Fãtiha*:7) Look at what has caused you trouble and kept you from joy: attachments, expectations, desires and fears—guard against these and you are already in the garden.

The root of the word *surûr* is also connected with the word meaning the cutting of the umbilical cord of a newborn baby. It is a joy because the child is no longer dependent on a thing called 'womb.' The cutting heralds his outer independence and leads him to the possibility of understanding that he is dependent only upon Allah. It is the beginning of a journey of joyfulness during which the child may begin to recognize that he is a child of Truth and Reality and that he is born by the grace of Allah, while the mother was the instrument within whom he had dwelt before birth. The potentiality of his existence before conception was in the knowledge of Allah and became an expression, a manifestation.

Sarîr (سرير , thrones, bed, singular of *surûr*) is a symbol of relief from outer troubles and a means of joy. It allows one to relax and establishes a mood of happiness, a state of restfulness. "Reclining on them, facing one another." Reclining upon the couches, the near ones are not troubled, they are relaxed. *Mutaqābilīn* (متقابلين ,facing one another) is from *taqābala* (تقابل), to meet, to be face to face. They see their reflection in each other. They see others who are like them. They see repeat performances, holograms. Its root is *qabala* (قبل), to receive; *qibla* (قبلة), from the same root, is that to which one turns; *qābila* (قابلة) is a midwife, the one who faces and receives the baby.

يَطُوفُ عَلَيْهِمْ وِلْدَانٌ مُّخَلَّدُونَ

17 **Round about them shall go youths never altering in age,**

بِأَكْوَابٍ وَأَبَارِيقَ وَكَأْسٍ مِّن مَّعِينٍ

18 **With goblets and ewers and a cup of pure drink:**

لَّا يُصَدَّعُونَ عَنْهَا وَلَا يُنزِفُونَ

19 **They shall not be affected with headache thereby, nor shall they get exhausted;**

وَفَاكِهَةٍ مِّمَّا يَتَخَيَّرُونَ

20 **And fruits such as they choose,**

وَلَحْمِ طَيْرٍ مِّمَّا يَشْتَهُونَ

21 **And the flesh of fowl such as they desire.**

This realm of experience, the *janna* (جنة , garden) is timeless. Man can only understand it from the reference point of his present existence which is based on existential needs, one person serving another. The *mithãl* (مثال , metaphor) of the eternally youthful servants implies that in the non time zone of the next life that state is no longer subject to decay.

The mentioning of meat in the garden is significant. It has been given its prominent position in this life because it is regarded as an important aspect of diet. It contains much of what man needs in terms of amino acids, minerals and vitamins. Traditionally, the practices of Islam encouraged the Muslims to eat it once or twice a week. Today, modern dieticians recommend that meat should only be eaten twice and fish once a week, the rest of the diet being composed of grains and vegetables. Traditionally, people ate animals that could be caught locally within the appropriate season. Today one finds people eating large quantities of meat and fat in places such as the Arabian peninsula where the temperature is exceedingly hot. Eating foods out of location and season only causes sickness. The *ãya* describing the availability of meat in the garden is a *mithal* and does not mean that there are hunting parties in the garden. The indication is that the nourishment is of the highest and subtlest values.

وَحُورٌ عِينٌ

22 **And pure, beautiful ones,**

كَأَمْثَالِ اللُّؤْلُؤِ الْمَكْنُونِ

23 **The like of the hidden pearls:**

جَزَآءًۢ بِمَا كَانُوا يَعۡمَلُونَ

24 **A reward for what they used to do.**

The *hûr* (حور ,virgins of paradise) are described as pearls, *maknûn* (مكنون ,hidden, kept, highly treasured; from the word *kanna* (كَنّ), to conceal, shelter. They are forever preserved in that translucency and purity.

The state of the garden is the mirror image, the reflection, of the quality of one's actions in this world. "A reward for what they used to do": one's reward is the action itself. It does not come later in time because in Reality there is no time. Action has its own reward within itself in this time zone. In the next life, where there is no time, it manifests again in meaning, in a state in which the soul sees itself.

Man perceives that having done a good turn for someone, he is paid back years later. Those with inner sight derive joy at the time of the action itself. They do not care for the visible outcome, which is completely secondary. It is like an expert gardener who, when he sees the plant nourished, visualizes the entire cycle of growth and decay. It is only the greedy and hungry fellow who simply waits for the fruit. The gardener who is totally in the joy of the process of gardening has already envisioned the fruit and has gone beyond it. Only the animal waits for the thing to manifest in order to eat it. From the point of view of the man of knowledge, the man who has abandoned himself, his action instantly contains the reward. And yet, there are also fruits that materially appear, but their unfoldment is in time and the seeker wants to know the non-time. It is the subtle being who recognizes that his action is its own reward. The quality of his reward is according to the source of his action, which is his intention. The being who has complete presence and awareness sees how the rewards and the actions are not separate.

لَا يَسْمَعُونَ فِيهَا لَغْوًا وَلَا تَأْثِيمًا

25 **They shall not hear therein vain or sinful discourse,**

إِلَّا قِيلًا سَلَٰمًا سَلَٰمًا

26 **Except the word peace, peace.**

Laghw (لغو ,foolish talk) is that which is empty of meaning. The root of the word is *laghã* (لغا) , to talk nonsense, to make mistakes; in another form (لغة), it means to invalidate, nullify, eliminate. From *laghã* comes the word *lugha*(لُغا), language. *Lughawî* (لغوى) means an expert in language and *laghwî* (لغوى) means someone who talks both a great deal and a lot of nonsense. Notice that an expert in language and one who talks nonsense are almost the same word.

"They shall not hear therein vain or sinful discourse." There is no *ta'thîm* (تأثيم), offense or sin. There is complete equity there, no injustice. Justice of the next world will be witnessed by all because there will be no interference with it. In this world one may see many outward aberrations in justice. Looking with an inner eye one sees nothing other than justice. As an outward being, having an outward orientation, one has to constantly do one's best to bring about outer justice, although inwardly one may see by the eye of abandonment that everything is perfect. Because there is no human interference, the next life will be completely meaningful and just. In this life, because man acts inadvertently or erroneously and transgresses, he recognizes what appears to be unjust. Looking through the eye of Reality, even what appears to be unjust is just.

Man is given a choice of acting or not acting. Acting wrongly results in an undesirable situation and therefore he makes claims of injustice. He has been acting incongruously with the governing laws. Outwardly, one strives to bring about outer justice; inwardly, one accepts whatever is decreed as being a part of the *tarbiya* (تربية ,upbringing), of the *rubûbiyya* (ربوبية , lordship). Outwardly, one acts as the hand of Allah, as the leg of Allah, as the eye of Allah, because man is the *khalîfa* (خليفه , deputy) of Allah. That is *tawhîd*. Man, being confused, usually acts in opposition to this because he is afraid of being tested.

If, in upholding justice, a man finds that he is swamped by a situation of injustice, he still does his best though it may engulf him. He realizes that the situation has been caused by the transgressions of others, but that he still must pay the price along with the others. Îmãn Husayn, *'alayhi-s-salãm*, did not escape the injustice that had been going on for twenty years. It cost his blood and that of seventy-two members of his family. He was not above it. The wave of tyranny will eat the good and the bad in its wake. But if a man is a true man of abandonment, he recognizes that this is the justice of Allah. He does not recognize his own he-ness. He too is part of the fodder.

Îmãn Hasan's fight was, in contrast, making a peace treaty. He knew that the forty thousand soldiers who were promised to him would turn against him on the day of battle, and he saw that there was no reason to shed blood. When he signed the treaty some people still turned against him. Whichever way one acts one cannot win with man's justice. Man's justice has flaws, while Allah's justice is perfect. Allah's justice is to give one the opportunity to know the meaning of blissful abandonment into Allah. By suffering the closing of all doors except one, man is guided to Allah's door.

"Except the word peace, peace." Peace is where there is no action, stillness beyond which there is no stillness, the eye of the storm where all is quiet. One minute in a hurricane seems like a year, whereas its eye appears to be in timeless peace. Its outer perimeter is in maximum agitation. The men of the state of the hurricane's eye, the people of the garden, do not hear any nonsense. There is no movement or anything other than recognizable, cognizable peace. It is not the peace of a dead stone but of pure awareness, a state of bliss which man can taste here and now if he keeps to the path of Allah, if he keeps to the path of the Qur'ãn and the *sunna* of the Prophet without hypocrisy. It is the higher state of the garden that men of Allah — who have taken the message and who have invested rightly, correctly and fully—can attain.

وَاَصۡحٰبُ الۡيَمِيۡنِ ۙ مَاۤ اَصۡحٰبُ الۡيَمِيۡنِ

27 **And the companions of the right hand; how happy are the companions of the right hand!**

فِىۡ سِدۡرٍ مَّخۡضُوۡدٍ

28 **Amid thornless lote-trees,**

For the "companions of the right hand," the state of joy that they had in this world is mirrored in the next. The *sidr* (سد ر) is the lote-tree of the next world. It has no thorns because everything in the next experience is in its purest form. Women are forever virginal, forever translucent, forever alive. Everything is in its ultimate, highest, purest, non-agitated form. Thorns are undesirable, and therefore do not exist in the garden of the next world. There is nothing that will afflict its inhabitants.

وَّطَلۡحٍ مَّنۡضُوۡدٍ

29 **And banana-trees (with fruits), one above another.**

Talhin mandûd (طلح منضود) is the description of the banana tree in the early stages of its development, when its clusters of fruit are bunched together. This is a reference to the fruits of different shapes and descriptions that may not have been known amongst people of the day. Arabia was limited in what it had of these items. It is an allusion to the fact that there are so many things which one does not know of in the next life, so many other aspects of taste or of realizations.

وَّظِلٍّ مَّمۡدُوۡدٍ

30 **And extended shade,**

وَّمَآءٍ مَّسۡكُوۡبٍ

31 **And water flowing constantly,**

وَّفَاكِهَةٍ كَثِيۡرَةٍ

32 **And abundant fruit,**

لَّا مَقۡطُوۡعَةٍ وَّلَا مَمۡنُوۡعَةٍ

33 **Neither intercepted nor forbidden,**

وَفُرُشٍ مَّرْفُوعَةٍ

34 **And exalted thrones.**

"And extended shade." In the desert culture of Arabia the sun, though a giver of life, is also a destroyer of life, so therefore shade is a great mercy. The bigger the shade of something the greater is the object itself, and what is greater than Allah, *al-Azim* (العظيم)? If you are with Allah you have maximum shade. *Zillin mamdûdin* (ظل ممدود) is literally a long or extended shadow. In Islamic culture one used to show respect to a revered person or saint by saying: "May Allah increase your shadow."

In the final abode one witnesses maximum shade. Everything is in the shade of the Creator. There are no individuals who can cast a shadow or darken anything. *Zillin mamdûdin* is the shadow which protects one and which, by inference, causes one to recognize Allah, because direct witnessing is not possible; one cannot see Reality, only its effects. The knowledge of Allah is by inference. One infers His existence. If anyone were to say that he has seen Allah, it would mean that he is either mad or a liar. If someone were to say that he has seen Allah at a given time and place, then where would He be the rest of the time? Allah is Ever-Present, All-Encompassing—beyond time, beyond comprehension, beyond sight. The faculties of sight and comprehension exist by the life which Allah has placed in people. How can these faculties perceive what makes them function? It is not possible. One infers there is Allah by reason, by heart, and by one's *fitra* (فطرة ,innate character). Within everyone is the seed that recognizes the perfect Creator. The imperfection in His creation that one sees is from the imperfect purification of one's own heart.

إِنَّآ أَنشَأْنَٰهُنَّ إِنشَآءً

35 **Surely We have made them to grow into a (new) growth,**

The garden is the new creation where there are no desires, whims, troubles or attachments. *Nasha'a* (نشأ) is to grow, to rise up, to come into existence. Allah says: "Surely We have made them to grow into a (new) growth." It is of another foundation, one that is not physical. It is based upon light. The world of light is only accessible to man in moments of deep meditation and reflection.

فَجَعَلْنَٰهُنَّ أَبْكَارًا

36 **Then We have made them virgins,**

عُرُبًا أَتْرَابًا

37 **Loving, equals in age,**

لِّأَصْحَٰبِ ٱلْيَمِينِ

38 **For the companions of the right hand.**

ثُلَّةٌ مِّنَ ٱلْأَوَّلِينَ

39 **A numerous company from among the first,**

وَثُلَّةٌ مِّنَ الْاٰخِرِيْنَ

40 **And a numerous company from among the last.**

Stretching man's imagination, Allah describes the physical satisfaction of man-woman companionship. "Then We have made them virgins." The women there, in the next experience, are in perpetual virginity. We understand that in this realm it is not possible. One of the Îmãns was asked how a woman could remain a virgin. He replied that it was not a question of virginity in the physical sense. The descriptions of women and drink are not what can be experienced or understood. They are a *mithãl*. They belong to another *inshã'* (انشاء), another construction in the world of lights and consciousness.

وَاَصْحٰبُ الشِّمَالِ ۙ مَا اَصْحٰبُ الشِّمَالِ

41 **And those of the left hand, how wretched are those of the left hand!**

فِيْ سَمُوْمٍ وَّ حَمِيْمٍ

42 **In hot wind and boiling water,**

وَّظِلٍّ مِّنْ يَّحْمُوْمٍ

43 **And the shade of black smoke,**

لَّا بَارِدٍ وَّلَا كَرِيْمٍ

44 **Neither cool nor honorable.**

Those at a loss in this world are grouped together and cast aside for their crimes. The beings that have not evolved and polished themselves in this existence are left to be recycled, fired and finished. They experience hot wind and boiling water, the opposites of tranquility, joy, stability and ease.

Allah's judgement is the perfect judgement. He is the All-Forgiving. He knows how to find and segregate those who are the doubtful cases. Some of the great seers, such as Mulla Sadra and Ibn al-'Arabi, often describe the situation of the 'in-between.' Although the zone of the 'in-between' begins in the next life, in the zone of non-time, its enactment can be imagined to be in time because it is the interspace, the 'in-between' of this life and the next, after the segregation.

Some of these seers talk about the purification of people by fire. Ibn al-'Arabi gives the fire seven different categories. A person may be put to fire in order to experience it, in order to give him a final chance to ask for forgiveness. Knowledge of the categories of fire may be of use, but may also result in unnecessary speculation. Being brought up in such a materialistic world, man immediately wants to subcategorize and contain everything, like the so-called scientists who run around the world collecting beautiful birds and butterflies to fill yet another biological museum. This is not the way to the attainment of inner knowledge. It is not by accumulation.

Traditions have reported that there are people who may be judged by men to be evil but by Allah's judgement are good. We cannot overlook someone's crime within *sharī'a* (شريعة , outward path); judgement in this zone of life can only be according to *sharī'a*, not beyond it. Allah will have His own judgement on the subtler, hidden aspects of transgression, but that is not our domain.

إِنَّهُمْ كَانُوا قَبْلَ ذَٰلِكَ مُتْرَفِينَ

45 **Surely they were before that made to live in ease and plenty.**

وَكَانُوا يُصِرُّونَ عَلَى الْحِنثِ الْعَظِيمِ

46 **And they persisted in the great violation.**

"Surely they were before that made to live in ease and plenty." *Mutraf* (مترف) means living luxuriously and recklessly in this world. It implies going beyond one's needs. Being reckless with nature's generosity, one becomes covetous and abusive. *Zakãt* (زكوٰة ,charity, purification by giving) acts as a natural cure against the greed that often besets man. The Prophet, *salla-llãhu 'alayhi wa ãlihi wa sallam*, was asked why *zakãt* was two and a half percent. He said that in following Allah's justice and nature's intention, one finds that for every thousand people there are twenty-five truly destitute ones who are unable to provide for themselves and have to be carried by the rest.

If Allah loves someone He causes him trouble so as to awaken him. Out of love for one's land one causes it trouble by ploughing it, turning it upside down. The business of the heart (قلب, *qalb*) is to be *maqlûb* (مقلوب , turned) so that it gives up and becomes free.

A *mutraf* loves the world and is content with it. Though the *mutraf* has invested wrongly, he is reinforced in his error by material success. The Qur'ãn advises the people of the right to leave him alone for his time will be short. He is far from Reality and unable to see that this life is going to come to an end. He has not invested in the next abode. Allah says that when He wants to destroy a culture or a people that have transgressed, He unleashes the *mutrafîn* (مترفين ,plural of *mutraf*). They know exactly how to manipulate the system. They are the ultimate parasites. By their transgression within the worldly system, justice is established. The ecology has a perfect mechanism of replenishing itself. The transgression of the *mutrafãn* will cause a reaction and they will be destroyed along with the elements and products of their transgression. It is a cybernetic, ecological cycle of destruction and self-rejuvenation, destroying an order that is not conducive to rejuvenate and resuscitate the order of nature. People are not destroyed by winged creatures descending and blowing fire on them. They are destroyed by the creature within and amongst themselves. Those who have a measure of detachment and reflection can see it repeated continuously in the history of man, because nothing changes. The *sunna* of Allah never changes. The law that governs existence is absolutely firm and is the foundation upon which everything else is built.

The permanency of the laws reflects an aspect of Allah's mercy, in that man is given something to rely upon. Man's laws have no such mercy or permanency. If the people who died a hundred years ago in America were to return, they would be imprisoned within a day, because they would have no idea of how to approach and negotiate the cumbersome, complicated laws of today. The true laws are unchanging laws. They come from the one and only true foundation of this existence and the next.

The *mutrafûn* often meet to decide about the billions in the world who are barely surviving. The well-off and those who are at ease discuss the plight of the have-nots in this world in an academic and abstract way. When the high-tech cultures study the ways and means of helping the have-nots, it is out of self-interest rather than out of equity and justice. They are concerned about poverty, because if it were left to become too widespread it could cause revolution and the loss of their potential markets. To stabilize the situation they make a token effort to help the poor in Indonesia, Malaysia, Bangladesh and Africa. The Qur'ãn says: "They persisted in great violation." The *mutrafûn* have persisted in violating the laws of Allah.

وَكَانُوْ يَقُوْلُوْنَ ۙ اَئِذَا مِتْنَا وَكُنَّا تُرَابًا وَّعِظَامًا ءَ اِنَّا لَمَبْعُوْثُوْنَ

47 **And they used to say: What! when we die and have become dust and bones, shall we then indeed be raised?**

اَوَ اٰبَآؤُنَا الْاَوَّلُوْنَ

48 **Or our fathers of yore?**

The deniers of the *akhira* (آخرة ,next life) think that this life is all that there is; therefore they want to grab all of it here and now in sensual pleasures and indulgences. There are two attitudes towards the next world. The first trusts that this world is not an end, but rather, a prelude to a never-ending world. Its people follow this trust until they know it directly. They are the believers. The man of trust regards this life as a training-ground for entry into the non-time zone. The second attitude towards the next world is held by the man without trust. He is greedy because there is nothing else for him but this life. He becomes increasingly covetous. He does not seek to obtain the qualifications for entry into the garden of the next life by sharpening his awareness, and increasing his joyfulness, abandonment and freedom. He is programmed to seek freedom but seeks it within the physical world. This is a perversion. Man is a seeker by nature, but if he believes that this life is the end, his motivation for action takes on a dimension that brings on chaos. This is the difference between the believer and the non-believer.

Man's disbelief in the *akhira* manifests in greed and aggressiveness. Today it is considered desirable to be aggressive and ambitious. In the past, if a person were described with those qualities, he would have been denounced. Now 'ambitious and aggressive' means he is the first candidate to be employed.

In every man there is a yearning to live forever. But he does not reflect that this yearning is from Allah beaming within him, telling him to come back to his source. It is a constant signal from the heart whose meaning is foreverness. Whatever good a man does, he will want to preserve forever. The call of Allah is from within, to come to know the meaning of foreverness, because He is the Forever. There is only He, *lã huwa illa hû* (لا هوالا هو , literally: There is no he but He). The point is missed, however, and the beam of light is dulled.

The world is attractive. Once you have dipped one toe in it you are pulled into its current and become completely engulfed. Human beings today are engulfed by the situation they are in. All are caught in the high-tech factory of modern life which does nothing other than spew them out after a lifetime of slave-like service, rejected and dejected. The best of them, their leaders, metamorphose into names of streets, stadiums and squares. The slaves follow habits, but the seeker breaks habits and becomes free of the system of enslavement.

قُلْ إِنَّ الْأَوَّلِينَ وَالْآخِرِينَ

49 **Say: The first and the last,**

لَمَجْمُوعُونَ ۙ إِلَىٰ مِيقَاتِ يَوْمٍ مَّعْلُومٍ

50 **Shall most surely be gathered together for the appointed hour of a known day.**

ثُمَّ إِنَّكُمْ أَيُّهَا الضَّالُّونَ الْمُكَذِّبُونَ

51 **Then shall you, Oh you who err and call it a lie!**

In the Qur'ãn, a day (يوم , *yawm*) does not mean twenty four hours. It is said that the day of your Lord is like a thousand years of what you count. Elsewhere it is described as fifty thousand years. With Allah there is no time. Time is relative, as is shown by the phenomenon of travelling near the speed of light. "The first and the last shall most surely be gathered together for the appointed hour of a known day." There is a specific destiny for the outer world and for the inner world.

Those who have denied continue in their state of loss, into the zone of the beyond-time where the time dimension is erased and a state of perpetual turmoil lasts forever. The denier, having denied that his breath was given to him in order to glorify the One Who gave him breath, finds it to be timeless restlessness. In the state of everlasting loss, in the fire, nothing takes root. The more one attempts to contain the fire, the more it devours what is in and around it.

لَآكِلُونَ مِن شَجَرٍ مِّن زَقُّومٍ

52 **Most surely eat of a tree of Zaqqum,**

فَمَالِئُونَ مِنْهَا الْبُطُونَ

53 **And fill (your) bellies with it;**

The individual is nourished from an everlasting bitterness, a tree of *zaqqûm* (زقوم) that comes up from the bottomless pit of *jahannam* (جهنم , hell). He experiences being lost in timelessness as if he was filling up his stomach with unnourishing bitterness. He drinks without satisfaction.

فَشَرِبُونَ عَلَيْهِ مِنَ الْحَمِيمِ

54 **Then drink over it of boiling water;**

فَشَرِبُونَ شُرْبَ الْهِيمِ

55 **And drink as drinks the thirsty camel.**

هَٰذَا نُزُلُهُمْ يَوْمَ الدِّينِ

56 **This is their gift on the day of requital.**

Water is used to extinguish and reduce heat and is one of the elements that seeks to establish equilibrium. These elements or characteristics are: wet, dry, hot, and cold. If one is too hot, one is likely to go towards what is cool. Being too dry attracts one towards the wet. Man seeks to be in balance. Everything is kept in balance by the One. But at the appointed hour, the characteristics of the elements which served as equalizers in the physical creation are no longer applicable. *Hîm* (هيم) are thirsty camels. This word is related to the word *hã'im* (هائم), meaning perplexed, mystified. In this life, man fills himself up with that which he considers necessary and without which he imagines he could not be happy. He abuses himself and nature by excessive consumption.

The description of the wretchedness of the "companions of the left" is that of *jahannam*, the fire. One of the derivatives of *jahannam* is *jahnîm* (جهنيم), a bottomless pit, the state of zero gravity, the state of receiving the very bad news that something you have cherished is no longer with you. Imagine someone suddenly being given news of multiple catastrophies, that everything which he had invested in, loved, or considered important for his tranquility, is gone—that is *Jahnim*.

Man wants *istiqrãr* (استقرار), which is constancy, stability, and security. One finds in Arabic that a word is linked to many other words through its root. These words echo variations, make clear, and give greater depth of meaning to the initial word. *Istaqarra* (استقرّ , verbal form of *istiqrãr*) is to seek security or permanent residence. *Iqrãr* (اقرار) is a foundation or settlement, and *qarrara* (قرّر) means to decide, report or relate. All these words belong to the same root as *qarra* (قرّ), which means to establish, determine or resolve.

If a man is a man of truthfulness, he must admit that he is, ultimately, secure; for how could he seek the foundation of the origin of something that was not already in him?

The fact that man is seeking security is the proof that his origin or essence is secure, but he is looking elsewhere in *ghafla*, (غفلة ,heedlessness, stupidity). He thinks that his security lies with this fellow or with that job—that is *ghafla*. The fact that he is looking for security means that security is naturally attainable.

There is a story about a man, who one night lost his ring and went looking for it under a street lamp. After some hours, while people had collected around him to help, no trace of the ring had been found. Someone finally asked where he had lost the ring and he replied, "I lost it in there," pointing to his house. "Why, then, are we not looking for it there?" asked the inquirer, shocked. The owner of the ring replied, "Because there is no light in there." Man often looks where it is convenient for him to search. He does not look where the truth lies. It is human nature.

نَحْنُ خَلَقْنَٰكُمْ فَلَوْلَا تُصَدِّقُونَ

57 **We have created you, why do you not then assent?**

أَفَرَءَيْتُم مَّا تُمْنُونَ

58 **Have you considered the seed?**

ءَأَنتُمْ تَخْلُقُونَهُۥٓ أَمْ نَحْنُ ٱلْخَٰلِقُونَ

59 **Is it you that create it or are We the creators?**

Man's coming forth into the world is not an accident, it is purposeful. Accident is a description used to indicate an inability to understand a situation. Man has been created, why can he not confirm that? Why can he not accept this as true? *Tusaddiqûn* (تصدقون) is from *saddaqa* (تصدّق), to consider to be true.

Can man not see how procreation occurs? Did he create his offspring or is he simply a vehicle? He has not a clue concerning the amazing transformation that takes place in the womb. It is by the act of Allah. His act is simply an animalistic act.

نَحْنُ قَدَّرْنَا بَيْنَكُمُ ٱلْمَوْتَ وَمَا نَحْنُ بِمَسْبُوقِينَ

60 **We have ordained death among you and We are not to be overcome.**

عَلٰى اَنْ نُّبَدِّلَ اَمْثَالَكُمْ وَنُنْشِئَكُمْ فِىْ مَا لَا تَعْلَمُوْنَ

61 **In order that We may bring in your place the likes of you and make you grow into what you know not.**

وَلَقَدْ عَلِمْتُمُ النَّشْاَةَ الْاُوْلٰى فَلَوْ لَا تَذَكَّرُوْنَ

62 **And certainly you know the first growth, why do you not then mind?**

"We have ordained death among you and We are not to be overcome." *Mawt* (موت), death, is the experience of an apparent discontinuity, a separation in the path. But man cannot experience separation unless he inherently contains the experience of gatheredness. The subtle entity within him separates from the gross entity and this separation is experienced as death. In the separation there is also unification. The body unifies with what it belongs to, its element. It goes back to the earth. The *rûh* (روح , spirit) goes back to where it belongs by the order of the one and only, all-permeating Creator. *Qadr* (قدر), from *qadara* (قدر), is what is ordained, decreed or measured. Everything is according to a measure.

When a culture is open, genuinely and spontaneously allowing for exposure, then it can grow, adapt and become fully fit. Then it is worthy of fulfilling its trust as the pinnacle of creation. When it is not, it is replaced. Cultures will come and go. There is an element of the survival of the fittest in every aspect of life, there is no denying it. Man has been brought here in a state which appears to be tarnished and which has the possibility of sinking low because of the necessary equilibrium between body and soul. He will be constructed again where the construction material is not physical. The next cycle in the rise of consciousness is based on material which is difficult for a human

—being constructed out of earth-bound, mud-made materials — to fully comprehend, except by a stretch of the imagination. Man is like a prisoner whose view is as wide as the bars on the windows of his cell allow. If he uses his faculties of reason and heart, he can imagine that what he sees in front of him must occur in likeness somewhere else. Through this use of perception man can reach an understanding of the *akhira*.

Understanding the first growth, man knows that biologically, he has come from a mucousy, base beginning. He knows in his heart, if the heart is *qãlib* (قالب , turning), that the root of life is not affected by his experiential life, but is a permanent, uncontaminated source. Allah appeals to man to look and understand that within him dwells the knowledge of his evolution, and that evolution, though manifesting now in time, must have had its roots in the zone of pre-creation. Man, from before creation, was planned. He was a potential manifestation. Allah reminds man in the Qur'ãn of the time when he was in the non-manifest, simply as potential energies.

أَفَرَءَيْتُم مَّا تَحْرُثُونَ

63 **Have you considered what you sow?**

ءَأَنتُمْ تَزْرَعُونَهُۥٓ أَمْ نَحْنُ ٱلزَّٰرِعُونَ

64 **Is it you that cause it to grow, or are We the causers of growth?**

لَوْ نَشَآءُ لَجَعَلْنَٰهُ حُطَٰمًا فَظَلْتُمْ تَفَكَّهُونَ

65 **If We pleased, We should have certainly made it broken down into pieces, then would you begin to lament:**

إِنَّا لَمُغْرَمُونَ

66 **Surely we are burdened with debt;**

"Have you considered what you sow?" Man is simply an instrument of sowing seeds, whether the seeds are those of other human beings or of plants. He is simply an actor. He has not written the script nor has he any possibility of changing the laws that govern it. The only degree of freedom he has is that of acting his role perfectly. When one sees a perfect actor, one believes that he is truly living his role. He has unified his will with destiny. It is an aspect of *tawhîd*; he genuinely and totally becomes one with his part. From Reality's point of view, he is not in separation though he may imagine that he is. If your act is pure and perfect then there is no resistance between your will and what you are applying yourself to, because the application has been for Allah, by Allah and in Allah. This is *baraka* (بركة , blessing), divine efficiency. It is harmony, ecology, balance and sanity.

Man is not the cause of events, he is simply one string of an instrument in an orchestra. Man can move because there is life in him. He did not cause life to come to him; he is only a conduit. If one is genuinely dependent on the knowledge that Allah is the best of guardians, then one truly knows that there is no power or strength except by Allah (*lã hawla wa la quwata illa billãh*), that Entity from Whom there has been no separation.

If Allah wills, the actions man may feel proud of may be destroyed. It is in man's nature that he will, with audacity and arrogance, explain as superficial causes what are actually and simply the will of Allah.

بَلْ نَحْنُ مَحْرُومُونَ

67 **Nay! we are deprived.**

The Qur'ãn carries the reader to the present, into the next life and into what preceded life. It is the unifier by a thread that goes back and forth in time.

"Surely, we are burdened with debt." *Gharama* (غرم) is to pay a fine. In physical existence man has fed himself from the wrong source and is now being penalized. The noun *gharãm*(غرام) means infatuation. When the final event occurs, at which time there is no possibility of arrogance or of duplicity, man is completely in a state of obsession and infatuation. There is no possibility of putting right his previous actions. If one thinks that he is in prison now, what will it be like then? No action will be rectifiable.

اَفَرَءَيْتُمُ الْمَآءَ الَّذِى تَشْرَبُونَ

68 **Have you considered the water which you drink?**

ءَاَنْتُمْ اَنْزَلْتُمُوهُ مِنَ الْمُزْنِ اَمْ نَحْنُ الْمُنْزِلُونَ

69 **Is it you that send it down from the clouds, or are We the senders?**

لَوْنَشَآءُ جَعَلْنَهُ اُجَاجًا فَلَوْ لَا تَشْكُرُونَ

70 **If We pleased, We would have made it salty;why do you not then give thanks?**

Look at the water you drink. If Allah had willed, all the water in the world could have been brackish. Reality challenges man by showing him the mercy and delicate balance of the creation. By changing one factor the entire creational setup would have been different; it would have been intolerant to forms of life on land. Taking for granted what Allah has given man is arrogance.

أَفَرَءَيْتُمُ النَّارَ الَّتِي تُورُونَ

71 **Have you considered the fire which you strike?**

ءَأَنتُمْ أَنشَأْتُمْ شَجَرَتَهَا أَمْ نَحْنُ الْمُنشِئُونَ

72 **Is it you that produce the trees for it, or are We the producers?**

Shajar (شجر) means tree. In Islamic culture the tree traditionally symbolizes the tree of life; its branches symbolize all the aspects of creation connected to one trunk which reaches down under the ground to its roots which draw up nourishment for the entire organism. Does man know the root of life? Does he know its meaning? Has he created it? Has he created fire? All that he has done is to rub two sticks together to get a spark; he has done nothing. He is simply an experiencer... Allah is the *Munshi'* (منشى), the Producer. Life's origin lies with the one and only Reality to Whom everything belongs anyway.

نَحْنُ جَعَلْنَاهَا تَذْكِرَةً وَمَتَاعًا لِّلْمُقْوِينَ

73 **We have made it a reminder and an advantage for the wayfarers of the desert.**

فَسَبِّحْ بِاسْمِ رَبِّكَ الْعَظِيمِ

74 **Therefore glorify the name of your Lord, the Great.**

Tadhkira (تذكرة) is from *dhikr* (ذكر), which is remembrance, awareness and a way of passage. *Tadhkira* in modern Arabic means a ticket. It is to remind whoever stops you at the gate that you are allowed to get into the next situation. It is the qualification for entry based upon reminding the ticket collector.

The password for the door to glorification is the Name, the *ism* (اسم). At the door, upon being received, the Name is given. A man of *sidq* (صدق), a man of truth, says: Allah, or, my Lord. It is said in the traditions that when the *ãya* "Therefore glorify the name of your Lord, the Great" came upon the Prophet, *salla-llãhu 'alayhi wa ãlihi wa sallam,* he made it the way of worship. He asked the Muslims to say, "*subhãna rabbi-l-'azîmi wa bihamdih*" when they went into *rukû'* (ركوع , bowing), because one does ruku after standing and witnessing this life, the next life, the fire, the garden, and the origin. Whoever praises the one and only Reality is heard, because Reality is the All-Knowing. Having done that, one falls down and obliterates one's profile. It is then, when one is at one's lowest, that one can speak of the Highest (الاعلى), *Al- A 'la—subhãna rabbi-l- A 'lã wa bihamdih*. In that state of obliteration the eyes are on dust, while one's inner eye sees the greatness of *Al- A 'lã*, the Highest, the Mightiest.

فَلَا أُقْسِمُ بِمَوَاقِعِ النُّجُومِ

75 **But nay! I swear by the falling of stars;**

وَإِنَّهُۥ لَقَسَمٌ لَّوْ تَعْلَمُونَ عَظِيمٌ

76 **And most surely it is a very great oath if you only knew;**

"But nay! I swear by the falling of the stars," means I swear by the truth of it, by the positioning of it. *Mawãqi'* (مواقع) position, place where something falls down) is from *waqa'a* (وقع), to fall. *Nujûm* (نجوم) are stars, or anything that has light—I swear by the light, by the self-effulgent light of this message, this spark of truth that ignites in the heart of the believer. The evidence is that the message hits the right switch in the heart and lights it up. Everyone is a star, different, yet the same. It is an oath of the truth of physical reality. It is an oath attesting to the perfection of the positions of all things in this creation. The fixed position of the stars are a manifestation of the order of the cosmos. These fixed positions are, in fact, dynamic. They are not rigid, but interact with their environment.

إِنَّهُۥ لَقُرْءَانٌ كَرِيمٌ

77 **Most surely it is an honored Qur'ãn,**

فِى كِتَٰبٍ مَّكْنُونٍ

78 **In a book that is protected;**

The Qur'ãn is that which is worthy of being read. It is that which has been gathered—the exposition of Reality. It encompasses what can be experienced and comprehended of Reality. It has immediate use in teaching one to live correctly, harmoniously and joyfully.

The Qur'ãn cannot be reached or understood if approached through the circumscribed limits of duality. If the reader is burdened by the affliction of duality, caused and nourished by his non-submission, then the Qur'ãn is veiled to him. As the pure exposition of Reality, the Qur'ãn can only reflect the degree of purity of the reader's heart.

لَّا يَمَسُّهُ إِلَّا الْمُطَهَّرُونَ

79 **None shall touch it save the purified ones.**

The Qur'ãn is subtle. It contains what man imagines can be contained and more. So how can one touch it? One can only come to know it if one stops knowing anything else, and by complete abandonment and submission lets go into the Qur'ãn—there is only the Qur'ãn. This is the essence of the meaning of Islam.

In the existential situation there is duality. Existential knowledge and information are based upon a seeker and a sought. Something that has a defined domain, such as a language, can be acquired. This is existential knowledge and is informative; it is based on time, thinking capacity, and patience. But the knowledge of Truth cannot be acquired in this fashion. It can only be acquired by allowing it to emerge, because it is already there rooted in the heart. The knowledge of Truth is not nourished because man nourishes everything else other than it. His energy has been diverted towards otherness, towards existential matters, and the self-effulgent knowledge of the Book has not been given its due attention. Truth is the substratum of existence and it upholds the cosmic event which man experiences in his short life.

تَنزِيلٌ مِّن رَّبِّ الْعٰلَمِينَ

80 **A revelation by the Lord of the worlds.**

Allah is the Lord of the two worlds, the physical and the non-physical—this world which man experiences, and the next world where he is subject to the effects of his previous intentions. He will experience and become his intentions, nothing more. In this world, the gross prevails over the subtle, while in the next the subtle becomes obvious and everything that was once hidden in one's heart becomes a *suhufan munashshara* (صحف منشرة), a spread-open book.

أَفَبِهَٰذَا الْحَدِيثِ أَنتُم مُّدْهِنُونَ

81 **Do you then hold this announcement in contempt?**

وَتَجْعَلُونَ رِزْقَكُمْ أَنَّكُمْ تُكَذِّبُونَ

82 **And to give (it) the lie you make your means of subsistence.**

The story of the *dunyã* (دنيا ,this material world) and the *ãkhîra* of this life and the next, is about purification. The human being can be likened to water which is by nature pure. As it flows it collects grains of sand. When the water is harnessed in a reservoir, the grains settle and the water reverts back to its pure nature. If the water is constantly kept in agitation the entire ecology of the water life is destroyed. Like water, human beings must harness themselves so that they can observe their wrong actions and avoid them. Otherwise their individual and societal ecologies will be disrupted and destroyed. The harness is the *'aql* (عقل, intellect, reason).

The moment the eternal absolute silence was broken by the rise of creation there was a tune. The song of *Îmãn* is the Qur'ãn and is continuously heard as growth moves on biologically. If we are not tuned to the song of *Îmãn*, we are tuned to other than it. If man is tuned to other than the Qur'ãn he will scorn the Qur'ãn, because he wants harmony, not discord. A receiver cannot pick up two signals at once and likewise man's nature is to listen to one waveband, not two.

فَلَوْلَا إِذَا بَلَغَتِ الْحُلْقُومَ

83 **Why is it not then that when it (soul) comes up to the throat,**

وَأَنتُمْ حِينَئِذٍ تَنظُرُونَ

84 **And you at that time look on**

وَنَحْنُ أَقْرَبُ إِلَيْهِ مِنكُمْ وَلَٰكِن لَّا تُبْصِرُونَ

85 **And We are nearer to it than you, but you do not see —**

Once man has committed himself to denial, he clings to it. He clings to what he has given value and invested in. When his life comes to an end, he is choked with death and held looking. Allah says: "And We are nearer to it than you, but you do not see." You have not been focusing your vision during your life on what is worthy of being seen. The Truth that permeates all manifestations is closer than closeness itself. That is the meaning of Allah's statement. The subtle power that underlies all visible powers is closer to the source, closer to Allah.

فَلَوْلَا إِن كُنتُمْ غَيْرَ مَدِينِينَ

86 **Then why is it — if you are not held under debt**

تَرْجِعُونَهَآ إِن كُنتُمْ صَٰدِقِينَ

87 **That you send it not back — if you are truthful?**

Dayn (دين), which means debt, is one side of a balance. If a man considers himself to be indebted, then obviously he will address himself to it correctly. If you consider yourself to be indebted to Reality then you will return that debt. The entire existence is based upon that debt about which Îmãm as-Sãdiq, *'alayhi-s-salãm*, asks how it can be repaid. It is not possible to repay it. For example, suppose you feel blissful as a result of a joyful moment and want to be thankful for your joy. When you bring to consciousness your thankfulness, you find then that you must be thankful for being able to thank, to thank endlessly, like the infinitely reflected images of two mirrors facing each other. This is the meaning, that there is no end to one's realization of the impossibility of paying such a debt. It is an unfathomable gift, and man squanders it.

"If you are not held under debt" is a question that cannot be challenged. Look at your life and how it has disappeared. Where are the controls that man thought he had? *'Ali Zayn ul-'Ãbidin, 'alayhi-s-salãm*, said: "The true *mu'm'in* (believer) dies as if he were taking off a filthy garment." But he who does not believe, and who has invested only in this world, has the garment of life torn and stripped from his being as he tries to cling on.

"Why is it—if you are not held under debt—That you send it not back—if you are truthful?" If you are not under debt, if you are not under the complete and utter control of your Lord, why then do you not send death back when it comes? The *mu'min*, upon hearing that somebody has died, says: "There is no power nor strength except by Allah." Man only has relative strength during the short period of his life.

The true seeker is heartened when he hears that somebody has died, because he knows death is the door to the next experience. He who believes rejoices, because the dead man is released from the confusion of the duality of this life, and with certainty now has knowledge. It is not that he rejoices because someone is destroyed—for it is only the flesh and the bones that are destroyed, the *rûh* lives on. The true seeker is interested in knowledge. When a baby is born, the true seeker cries, knowing what this new entity will have to go through.

فَأَمَّآ إِن كَانَ مِنَ الْمُقَرَّبِينَ

88 **Then if he is one of those drawn nigh (to Allah),**

فَرَوْحٌ وَرَيْحَانٌ وَجَنَّتُ نَعِيمٍ

89 **Then happiness and bounty and a garden of bliss.**

"Then if he is one of those drawn nigh (to Allah)." Man does not know the Real. He does not know the way to the Real because there is no way to the Real. But he may come to know what is not the Real. He learns the roads that take him far from Reality. By stopping the drives along those roads one can naturally and spontaneously be on the one and only road, the one and only path of tawhîd. The worldly existence and the next life of he who is close to Allah is one of *na'îm* (نعيم), comfort and ease, which is the *janna* (جنة ,garden of paradise). In it he sees things with *tawhîd* and is not subject to experiential changes.

The Prophet *'Îsa, 'alayhi-s-salãm*, said: "I was looking for my people when I came across those who were afraid of the fire. I told them, 'You will win by your trade. But that is not what I am looking for.' Then I came upon the people who were praying for the garden and I said to them, 'You will get it but you are enslaved to that state. I am not looking for that.' Then I came upon people who were truly and simply in worship, in sane bewilderment, in pure glorification, and I said to them, 'You are my people.'

If you want Allah, the fire and the garden are the steps to Him. In the Qurãn there are descriptions of their different degrees. The final degree of the garden is where there is no sound and nothing is heard: "They shall not hear therein vain or sinful discourse, except the word peace, peace." If there is anything to be heard it is peace, peace. It is pure consciousness. What happens in the lower garden is the negation, or the neutralization, of desires by their fulfillment, in order for one to go beyond them into utter silence, into the essence.

وَأَمَّا إِن كَانَ مِنْ أَصْحٰبِ الْيَمِينِ

90 **And if he is one of those on the right hand,**

فَسَلٰمٌ لَّكَ مِنْ أَصْحٰبِ الْيَمِينِ

91 **Then peace to you from those on the right hand.**

This *sûra* is about the different states that one may acquire according to the degree of one's *tawhîd*. The *muqarrabûn* (مقربون), the close ones, are far from other than Him and are therefore close to Him.

The people of the right are the righteous, are those who have acted diligently. Some commentators describe the *ashãbu-l-yamîn* (اصحاب اليمين ,companions of the right) as the *ashãbu-l-mujãhada* (اصحاب المجاهدة), the people who are in *jihãd*

(جهاد) , the people who continually strive and are patient in their suffering. There is peace upon them even though they are in turmoil and affliction. This life is the house of affliction, but if the affliction is harnessed along the path taken by the Prophet, *salla-llāhu 'alayhi wa ālihi wa sallam,* it is tolerable. Otherwise a sane person can only jump from a window and openly declare the incomprehensibility of his existence. This life is a place of hardship in which resistance to Allah's mercy is rubbed away. Man has no option but to be in *jihād*.

وَأَمَّا إِنْ كَانَ مِنَ الْمُكَذِّبِينَ الضَّالِّينَ

92 **And if he is one of the rejecters, the erring ones,**

فَنُزُلٌ مِّنْ حَمِيمٍ

93 **He shall have a gift of boiling water,**

وَتَصْلِيَةُ جَحِيمٍ

94 **And burning in hell.**

"And if he is one of the rejecters," meaning, if he has denied the one and only Truth, if he has denied that *tawhīd*. A man by his rejection is called one of the *mukadhdhibin ad-dāllīn* (مكذبين الضالين , rejecters, erring ones). First he lies, denying what he knew within his heart to be true. If man denies his indebtedness, he is at a loss.

"He shall have a gift of boiling water." Man can experience the drinking of hot water here and now. When one becomes very angry and emotionally disturbed, even attempts to crush that anger are rejected and only increase the fire of agitation. The cool rains of mercy are not recognized and thus have the effect of boiling water. An outer fire is containable and its boundaries are known, while the inner fires of desire, lust, fear and anger, are without boundary. Man himself is the tree that feeds the fire. The ultimate state of the *mukadhdhibin* becomes *nuzulun min hamîm* (نزل من حميم). Their home is where the boiling water, the fire, is. They dwell in *jahîm* (جحيم), roasting hell.

إِنَّ هٰذَا لَهُوَ حَقُّ الْيَقِينِ

95 **Most surely this is a certain truth.**

فَسَبِّحْ بِاسْمِ رَبِّكَ الْعَظِيمِ

96 **Therefore glorify the name of your Lord, the Great.**

"Most surely this is a certain truth." One is earning entry into the next life by one's actions in this life—and actions are based on intentions. Man manufactures either the key to hell or the key to heaven, and begins to experience those states here by the purity of his intentions. There is no discontinuity. Those who manufacture the key to hell already experience it now. It is a continuum from this life into the next.

The one who manufactures the key of joy, the key to the garden, has already entered that state. The file that he has in his hand, which is knowledge combined with action, is used to smooth the rough edges of himself, of his personality, with all its special contours of desire. If he is ultimately willing to be filed down to nothing, to be a non-entity, then he will recognize the One Entity. The more he asserts his own identity, the less he can see the One Entity.

The Prophet, *salla-llãhu 'alayhi wa ãlihi wa sallam*, has said: "There are not two hearts in the breast of man." If one's intention is to know, one will come to know Allah. And once you have come to know Allah, nothing else matters. If your intention is only to have economic well-being, then you will get that and all the difficulties inherent in it. If your intention is to have a house and the pleasure of children, you will get that and the disappointments that naturally come along with it. You cannot get one thing without its opposite. This is the balance. The Qur'ãn is called the *Mizan* (الْمِيزانُ), the Balance, and the laws that govern existence are in balance. Existence is not chaos, it is cosmos—in precise balance.

Amîr ul-Mu'minîn 'Ali, *'alayhi-s-salãm*, once said that the first thing that comes to the man of abandonment and faith is a glimpse of Reality, of which he seeks to attain certainty. That certainty comes by questioning,, studying, understanding, and moving steadily along the path, by living the Qur'ãn. The first stage of certainty is like being informed that there is a fire in the wood, and you trust the reliability of the informant to have given correct information. This is called *'ilmu-l-yaqîn* (علم اليقين ,the knowledge of certainty). The second stage is actually seeing it, witnessing the truth of the message, and this is *'aynu-l-yaqîn* (عين اليقين , the eye or source of certainty). The third stage is *haqqu-l-yaqîn* (حق اليقين , the truth of certainty), which is actually experiencing the fire. One experiences the fire's warmth by being next to it or being burned by it. There is no doubt about its quality anymore. The fourth stage is *haqqu-l-haqq* (حق الحق , the truth of the truth), when one is consumed in the fire and there is nothing left.

Lã huwa illa hû: There is none other than He. This is the final stamp of Truth. One burns in it. Nothing can take it away from you once it has been engraved because then you have paid your debt.

Having received the message, all that the believer can do is glorify—by His permission, by entry through that door, by the name of Allah—the divine, all-encompassing, higher consciousness; the Greatest, the Highest and the Mightiest. Pronouncing His name means one neglects other names, other labels. The believer trusts that he will come to enter that state, into the house of Allah; calling upon Allah, wandering into the fields of confusion, calling and calling, until he wakes up. Then he finds that he was in the house of Allah all the time, but was veiled from this knowledge only by his imagination.

سُورَةُ الْمُلْكِ مَكِّيَّة (٦٧)
وَآيَاتُهَا ثَلَاثُونَ

SURAT UL-MULK

THE KINGDOM

Introduction

This Makkan *sûra* illustrates and proves the comprehensive totality of lordship. Creation appears to be made of different systems, each moving towards the fulfillment of its potential, and these systems, seen or unseen, are interlinked.

The Controller of all these systems is one Creator Who is beyond time and encompasses all of creation. All bounties and mercies are for the purpose of recognizing His unbounded mercy, the mercy of this beneficent Creator to Whom all creation will return, and by Whose grace creation has come about.

بِسْمِ اللّٰهِ الرَّحْمٰنِ الرَّحِيْمِ

In the name of Allah, the Beneficent, the Merciful.

تَبٰرَكَ الَّذِى بِيَدِهِ الْمُلْكُ ز وَهُوَ عَلٰى كُلِّ شَىْءٍ قَدِيْرٌ

1 **Blessed is He in Whose hand is the kingdom,**
and He has power over all things,

الَّذِى خَلَقَ الْمَوْتَ وَالْحَيٰوةَ لِيَبْلُوَكُمْ اَيُّكُمْ اَحْسَنُ عَمَلاً ط وَهُوَ الْعَزِيزُ الْغَفُورُ

2 **Who created death and life that He may try you—which of you is best in deeds; and He is the Mighty, the Forgiving,**

The creation is based on the Creator's love for what He created. And what He created was from Him, sustained by Him, supported by Him, to Him. When that love is made manifest to the created, he tastes joy and blessedness. The source and transmission of that joy and blessedness exist at all times. It is only the created who inadvertently block it. The entire creation is a result of the blessedness of He Whose creation is His kingdom. Everything in it is in His hand and comes from His power. Every creational entity, therefore, derives its power directly from the Creator.

Allah created the experiences of life and death. In this life, man is put into situations in order to be purified of any additions which are perversely taken on. The *balã'* (بلاء , affliction) is a necessary test which moves him, with knowledge, into higher degrees of purity. Affliction (بلوى , *balwã*) is his means of eliminating the barrier of desires and expectations existing between himself and the Creator. Affliction teaches the created being to live freely, acknowledging the gift of life given to him. The best of actions are those which are done with no expectations. They are purely and simply *fĩ sabĩli-llãh* (فى سبيل الله , for the sake of Allah).

The first manifestation of creation is life. The experience of life is meaningful only if there exists its opposite, the experience of death. These experiences are such that everyone goes through them. Just as there is outer life and death, so is there inner life and death. When the heart is hardened it is as if dead. When it is flowing and turning, it is alive. Life and death exist in both the sensory and in the meaning.

"And He is the Mighty, the Forgiving." Whether or not man is content with his life does not change Allah's station with him. Through afflictions, growth of wisdom blossoms in him. Man learns to solicit forgiveness from the *Ghafãr* (الغفور ,the Forgiving). The recognition of one's transgressions and mistakes is in itself a door to forgiveness. If one knows one's faults, if one has seen them and experienced them, then one is on the way to being forgiven. It follows that if one is in awareness, one will be unlikely to repeat past mistakes.

الَّذِى خَلَقَ سَبْعَ سَمٰوٰتٍ طِبَاقًا ط مَاتَرٰى فِى خَلْقِ
الرَّحْمٰنِ مِنْ تَفٰوُتٍ ط فَارْجِعِ الْبَصَرَ هَلْ تَرٰى مِنْ فُطُوْرٍ

3 **Who created the seven heavens one above another; you see no incongruity in the creation of the Beneficent God; then look again, can you see any disorder?**

ثُمَّ ارْجِعِ الْبَصَرَ كَرَّتَيْنِ يَنْقَلِبْ اِلَيْكَ الْبَصَرُ خَاسِئًا
وَّهُوَ حَسِيْرٌ

4 **Then turn back the eye again and again; your look shall come back to you confused while it is fatigued.**

The kingdom of Allah is manifest in seven layers, seven different phases or modes of heaven. Each layer is placed upon another, invisibly connected yet retaining its own characteristics. It is also found amongst the *ahãdîth* (احاديث , prophetic traditions) and the sayings of the Imãms that the earth has seven layers. In fact, there is a common supplication in which it is said: *Rabbu-s-samawãti-s-sab 'i wa rabbu-l-arãdini-s-sab'i'*, the Lord of the seven heavens and the Lord of the seven earths.

"You see no incongruity in the creation of the Beneficent God." *Futûr* (فطور) is from *fatara* (فطر), to cleave, split open. *Fitra* (فطرة) is the original crack—the origin of man's rise to life. The *Rahmãn* (الرحمان ,the Merciful) encompasses everything under His *rahma* (رحمة ,compassion). Allah's *rahma* is upon all creation, while His *rahm* is upon the *mu'min* (مؤمن ,believer). Under the *Rahmãn*, the Merciful, there is nothing in creation that cannot be placed. There is no disjointedness within it. Everything makes sense to man if he develops the right sight and abandons clumsy judgement. Allah says "Then turn back the eye again and again," because though man looks often, he does so without insight. The Qur'ãn challenges man to look again in order to see if he can find any fault. The more one looks, the more one discovers the perfection of what appears to be layer upon layer of the laws and sensory connections which hold the cosmos together.

Doubt arises in man when he begins to reflect. At first, his reflections are unclear and do not connect with his core. But the more he reflects, the more likely it becomes that he will see the pure mercy that will bring him realization and understanding. Sight will come back to him and he will be unable to find fault.

"Your sight shall come back to you spurned while it is fatigued." *Khãsi'* (خاسئ) means spurned, base, vulgar, rejected. *Hasîr* (حصير) means exhausted, desperate or fatigued. If he reflects, man will not be able to see fault. His sight will show nothing other than the *Rahmãn* Whose manifestation is in the complete perfection of His creation. There will be nothing out of place. Creational entities will interconnect in the most precise manner. It will confirm that the All-Pervading manifests His *rahma*. In other words, man's faculty of reason and insight will come to see the perfection of creation.

وَلَقَدْ زَيَّنَّا السَّمَآءَ الدُّنْيَا بِمَصَابِيحَ وَجَعَلْنٰهَا رُجُومًا
لِّلشَّيٰطِينِ وَاَعْتَدْنَا لَهُمْ عَذَابَ السَّعِيرِ

5 **And certainly We have adorned this lower heaven with lamps and We have made these missiles for the Shaytāns, and We have prepared for them the chastisement of burning.**

وَلِلَّذِينَ كَفَرُوا بِرَبِّهِمْ عَذَابُ جَهَنَّمَ ۖ وَبِئْسَ الْمَصِيرُ

6 **And for those who disbelieve in their Lord is the punishment of hell, and evil is the resort.**

اِذَآ اُلْقُوا فِيهَا سَمِعُوا لَهَا شَهِيقًا وَّهِيَ تَفُورُ

7 **When they shall be cast herein, they shall hear a loud moaning of it as it heaves,**

تَكَادُ تَمَيَّزُ مِنَ الْغَيْظِ ۖ كُلَّمَا اُلْقِيَ فِيهَا فَوْجٌ سَاَلَهُمْ
خَزَنَتُهَآ اَلَمْ يَاْتِكُمْ نَذِيرٌ

8 **Almost bursting for fury. Whenever a group is cast into it, its keeper shall ask them: Did there not come to you a warner?**

قَالُوا بَلٰى قَدْ جَآئَنَا نَذِيْرٌ ۙ فَكَذَّبْنَا وَقُلْنَا مَا نَزَّلَ اللّٰهُ
مِنْ شَىْءٍ اِنْ اَنْتُمْ اِلَّا فِىْ ضَلٰلٍ كَبِيْرٍ

9 **They shall say: Yea! indeed there came to us a warner, but we rejected (him) and said: Allah has not revealed anything; you are only in a great error.**

وَقَالُوا لَوْ كُنَّا نَسْمَعُ اَوْ نَعْقِلُ مَا كُنَّا فِىْ اَصْحٰبِ
السَّعِيْرِ

10 **And they shall say: Had we but listened or pondered, we should not have been among the inmates of the blazing fire.**

The lower heaven is that heaven which is perceivable by man. The other heavens, it is implied, are beyond visible recognition. They are based on energies or subtle forces that hold the cosmos together. The stars decorate the lower heaven, which displays myriads of dynamic exchanges, whether seen or inferred by observation.

"And certainly we have adorned this lower heaven with lamps and we have made these missiles for the *shaytãns*." *Rajama* (رجم), the root of the word for missiles, is to stone, curse. There are several meanings that can be given to this phrase. One is that the evil unseen forces of *shaytãn* (شيطان,satan) cannot penetrate beyond the lower heaven. Another meaning is that it indicates that those people who use supernatural powers and magic are afflicted and are unable to penetrate beyond a limit.

All forms of *shaytãn* or deviation lead one to the *'adhãbu-s-sa'îr* (عذاب السعير), the chastisement of the blazing fire. Those who are in the state of *shaytãn* --- denying the Lordship, covering up, disbelieving in the fact that there is a Sustainer by whom we are guided to our fullest possibilities—will earn the state of eternal fire, than which there is nothing worse. *Masîr* (مصير), a place of arrival or final destiny, comes from *sãra* (صار), which means to become, implying 'timeness.'

The sighing or moaning that is uttered when a being enters *jahannam* (جهنم ,hell) is a final expression called *shahîq* (شهيق, sighing, sobbing). *Shahaqa* (شهق) means to inhale, sigh deeply, gulp, moan. When in the final abode, beings emit the sound of mourning in an environment which is forever changing, never sustaining or stabilizing—the reverse of *janna* (جنة , paradise).

In the ever effulgent fire, churning and turning with its anger, increasing as it is fed, a voice reflects or a memory comes forth to ask:Were you not informed about this state? Were you not warned that you were preparing yourself for this dreadful end? The questioners are the keepers of the fire, its permanent angels or guardians.

Those who are questioned answer: We did not hear. We denied the existence of Reality. We denied Allah. We ascertained that there was no Reality and assumed those who were reflecting the voice of Truth to be in error.

There is nothing other than justice in this world and the next. If man does not hear the voice of wisdom which will guide him in this world and show him how to live in a manner that will keep him from harm—if he does not heed that wisdom, he will be afflicted in this life. But there is a higher state, one in which there is belief in and recognition of Allah. If that state does not come about, the punishment will be both in this world and the next—when relative time stops and absolute timelessness begins.

This is not theatrical language. There is instantaneous, out-of-time communication between entities. In this life the deniers put up a barrier between the faculty of hearing and that of understanding what can be heard. They block the exercise of the natural faculty of reason, that innate sense with which everyone is endowed. They misinterpret for the sake of convenience, sentimental attachment, or emotionalism, or for the love of the *dunyā* (دنيا , world in a negative material sense).

فَاعْتَرَفُوا بِذَنۢبِهِمْ فَسُحْقًا لِّأَصْحَـٰبِ السَّعِيرِ

11 **So they shall acknowledge their sins, but far will be (forgiveness) from the inmates of the blazing fire.**

"So they shall acknowledge their sins." *I'tarafû* (اعترفوا), derives from *'arafa* (عرف), to know; *I'tarafa* (اعترف) is to admit, confess or acknowledge. At the time of the punishment, there is a natural confession. Those who are to be punished will admit that they have hidden themselves from the messages brought to mankind by the prophets, their followers and the Imāms (leaders). Everyone has the ability to discern the truth and is therefore able to acknowledge that he has original knowledge. But man hides and denies it through his ignorance, which is built upon arrogance, fear, anxiety and attachment.

Bali-l- insānu 'ala nafsihi basīra: "Nay, man is evidence against himself." (*al-Qiyāma*:14) Everyone has within himself a higher awareness which can shed light on his consciousness. If his consciousness is impure, then his higher awareness is able to discern that his consciousness is dwelling upon something unbecoming. Even so, man can still deny the reflection of his higher awareness. At the point of death, when the ability to interfere with one's destiny stops, all instantaneously becomes clear because time stops.

"But far will be (forgiveness) from the inmates of the burning fire." *Sahaqa* (سحق) means to crush, annihilate, pulverize. The people of the fire are those who are obliterated by not having acknowledged the one and only Entity—Allah. How can they remain whole? If one does not admit the power of an ordinary king, he will be crushed. How much more important is it then to accept the One and All-Powerful, Whose kingdom is pervaded by Him. Because of His mercy He gives man countless chances throughout his life to help save himself from the fire.

إِنَّ الَّذِينَ يَخْشَوْنَ رَبَّهُم بِالْغَيْبِ لَهُم مَّغْفِرَةٌ وَأَجْرٌ كَبِيرٌ

12 **(As for) those who fear their Lord in secret, they shall surely have forgiveness and a great reward.**

"(As for) those who fear their Lord in secret, they shall surely have forgiveness and a great reward." The *ghayb* (غيب) is the Unseen. Those who have accepted the fact that there is a Creator, a Reality, without direct personalized evidence—without witnessing it—have taken it on by the inference that there cannot be an effect without a cause. They have directly experienced that there are laws that govern this existence and that the cosmos is not in chaos. They want to know the laws—they fear their Lord and they fear transgressing His laws, His bounds. It is for them that there is forgiveness and a great reward, a continuing reward that begins here in this world and continues uninterruptedly into the next.

وَاَسِرُّوْاقَوْلَكُمْ اَوِ اجْهَرُوْابِهٖ ط اِنَّهٗ عَلِيْمٌۢ بِذَاتِ الصُّدُوْرِ

13 **And conceal your word or manifest it; surely He is Cognizant of what is in the hearts.**

Asirrû (اسّروا) is from *asarra* (اسرّ), meaning to keep secret, to conceal or disguise something. Whether one speaks of it or not, whether one hides it or not, whether one reveals what is inside oneself or not, Allah is aware of what goes on within the heart. *Sadr* (صدر) means chest, heart or front. Reality knows what man has put in front of himself, what he has put foremost in his heart. Already, even in this life, there is no hiding place; man is exposed.

The creator of a thing knows its attributes. The creator of a house knows its strengths and weaknesses. He knows the materials he used to build it, what appears on the walls and what is behind the walls. The merciful Perfect-Builder has built with perfection. He has not placed poor quality material behind the walls. Behind the wall of the chest of man He has placed a heart. It is in the hearts of men that He dwells.

اَلَا يَعْلَمُ مَنْ خَلَقَ ط وَهُوَ اللَّطِيْفُ الْخَبِيْرُ

14 **Does He not know, Who created? And He is the Knower of the subtleties, the Aware.**

"And He is the Knower of the Subtleties, the Aware." Subtlety is all-pervading. All entities are plugged into life through the subtle forces of the Creator. The ordinary electrical machine must be plugged into a physical outlet, but Allah's outlet is the entirety of space on earth. As man moves he is spontaneously plugged into the Source. How can one deny the existence of the Creator and that everyone is under His mercy? Allah holds the knowledge and the power of deciding who will remain plugged into the life-support system and whose body is to go back to the worms.

This life is like a laboratory in which the Creator tests the fidelity of His creations. He experiments with them, allowing them to transgress, and gives them the chance to correct themselves. Having made a mess of their lives, they are allowed to wash themselves completely clear of their actions. Many *ahādîth* (plural of *hadîth*, tradition) refer to certain acts of worship, such as *haj* (حج, pilgrimage to Makkah), which, if performed correctly, are like a rebirth. The prayers of the Muslim, if done correctly, make the worshipper emerge refreshed and renewed. None of the negativeness of his past affects him, and all his experiences, the wisdom of a lifetime, are at his disposal.

هُوَ الَّذِى جَعَلَ لَكُمُ الاَرْضَ ذَلُولاً فَامْشُوا فِى
مَنَاكِبِهَا وَكُلُوا مِن رِّزْقِهِ ط وَإِلَيْهِ النُّشُورُ

15 **He it is Who made the earth smooth for you; therefore go about in the spacious sides thereof, and eat of His sustenance, and to Him is the return after death.**

ءَاَمِنتُم مَّن فِى السَّمَآءِ اَن يَّخسِفَ بِكُمُ الاَرْضَ
فَإِذَا هِىَ تَمُورُ

16 **Are you secure of those in the heaven that He should not make the earth to swallow you up? Then lo! it shall be in a state of commotion.**

أَمْ أَمِنتُم مَّن فِي السَّمَآءِ أَن يُرْسِلَ عَلَيْكُمْ حَاصِبًا ط
فَسَتَعْلَمُونَ كَيْفَ نَذِيرِ

17 **Or are you secure of those in the heaven that He should not send down upon you a punishment? Then shall you know how was My warning.**

وَلَقَدْ كَذَّبَ الَّذِينَ مِن قَبْلِهِمْ فَكَيْفَ كَانَ نَكِيرِ

18 **And certainly those before them rejected (the truth), then how was My disapproval.**

In order for man to have the opportunity to express and experience his faith and sincerity, the earth has been made *dahalûl* (زلول , smooth, gentle, easy); upon it he seeks wisdom and *rizq* (رزق , provision, sustenance, divine blessing).

"To Him is the return after death." *Nushûr* (نشور , Resurrection) comes from *nashara* (نشر), to announce, spread out, make known, and to resurrect, return from the death. *Nashir* (نشير) is a publisher. Allah is the supreme publisher, making known His creation. The earth, with its massive mountains, has been made low and submissive. Allah has made the earth smooth so as to be accessible for man to tread upon, indicating the ease that may come from what appears to be difficulty. *Manãkib* (مناكب) are the shoulders, flanks or highlands; they are what are difficult to tread upon. But Allah has made man able to travel upon the earth's 'shoulders.' It is an encouragement for man to seek the means to glorify Allah, seeking provision wherever it may easily come forth in this spacious and varied land.

How can one be secure from He Who is in the heavens and is the King of all? There is no certainty that the earth will remain still and not suffer an earthquake. Can one be certain of the earth's solidity? The *mu'min* is in perpetual awareness, knowing that if he allows himself to think that he is secure from change, he is lost. He trusts that Allah will guide him through the approaching changes and afflictions. Allah says elsewhere in the Qur'ãn: *fa-lã ya'manû makra-llahi illa-l-qawmu-l-khãsirun*: "But none of those feels secure from Allah's plan except the people who shall perish." (*al- A 'rãf*:99).

The earth is Allah's laboratory, in which man's attainment is measured according to his commitment to service. It would be unfair if man were suddenly exposed to knowledges that he was not ready to receive. It would be shattering and unnatural. Therefore, there is greater responsibility with additional knowledge.

The relationship of knowledge, responsibility, and Allah, the Giver of knowledge, may be likened to the relationship of the father to his son. The father out of love for his son, measures the degree of his willingness to take on responsibility by testing him. He does not wish to afflict the boy, but recognizes that the more one knows the more one is burdened. For example, being aware of A bird tests its young to see whether or not it can fly from its nest. The mother does not immediately push the chick over the edge, but nudges it, encouraging it to use its wings until they grow in strength. The young bird realizes that it is free as it leaps out of the nest and into the air.

Man is, in reality, free of other than Allah. Allah is unlimited, so man is free beyond limit, but he does not know this because he has not used the wings of *îmãn* (ايمان ,faith, trust) and complete dependence upon Allah.

The uncertainty of events stimulates us to reflect in order to be in true abandonment—aware and alive in the now, second by second. In His love for man, Allah tightens His rope upon him for a moment. The rope reminds him of Allah at that instant, but Allah is present all the time. If man is a deserving slave, if he admits to the nobility of his Creator, then he is a noble creation. A noble horse does not have to constantly be pulled and hit on the head, it spontaneously knows that it has a master. Likewise, if man is jolted every now and then it is because he has gone off course—that is the proof of the love of the One Who holds the reins.

One can never be sure to which network of laws one is subjecting oneself. It is man, by his actions and intentions, who unifies himself with a certain set of laws. If his actions are honest and sincere, emanating from a pure source, then he is in a river whose end product and destiny is quite clear. On the other hand, because of man's situation and the degree of his *kufr* (كفر ,denial) and unconnectedness, he will be brought into a stream in which he will see an increasing amount of disjointedness and be subjected to an increasing amount of shattering.

The individual's journey in this life is like being in a hovercraft that is skimming across hundreds of different rivers, which are the laws of destiny. The passenger, according to his intention, puts his foot into one river or another. The choice is his. If out of ignorance he puts his foot into a river of filth and danger, then all that he can do is to pull it out, climb back into his vehicle, and move on to the next river. These laws, these rivers, govern destiny. It is up to the individual to end up in the river that gives him smooth passage and genuinely reflects the truth of the Merciful behind it.

اَوَلَمْ يَرَوْا اِلَى الطَّيْرِ فَوْقَهُمْ صٰٓفّٰتٍ وَّ يَقْبِضْنَ ط
مَايُمْسِكُهُنَّ اِلَّا الرَّحْمٰنُ ط اِنَّهٗ بِكُلِّ شَىْءٍ بَصِيْرٌ

19 **Have they not seen the birds above them expanding (their wings) and contracting (them)? What is it that withholds them save the Beneficent God? Surely He sees everything.**

اَمَّنْ هٰذَا الَّذِىْ هُوَ جُنْدٌ لَّكُمْ يَنْصُرُكُمْ مِّنْ دُوْنِ الرَّحْمٰنِ ؕ اِنِ الْكٰفِرُوْنَ اِلَّا فِىْ غُرُوْرٍ

20 **Or who is it that will be a host for you to assist you besides the Beneficent God? The unbelievers are only in deception.**

اَمَّنْ هٰذَا الَّذِىْ يَرْزُقُكُمْ اِنْ اَمْسَكَ رِزْقَهٗ ج بَلْ لَّجُّوْا فِىْ عُتُوٍّ وَّنُفُوْرٍ

21 **Or who is it that will give you sustenance if He should withhold His sustenance? Nay! they persist in disdain and aversion.**

Reflect upon what is above us in the form of birds. Nothing holds them up. The explanations given for this natural phenomenon are simply that, explanations; they are not the truth. Man tries to explain the flight of bird and airplane with a narrow band of counter-balanced mathematical forces. Tons of steel are in the airplane—how does it fly? How does it hang in the air? A steel ship floats upon water—what do these phenomena mean? Allah manifests Reality in this existence in wondrous ways. Nothing holds the bird up except the mercy of Allah. The mercy of Allah allows us to see all these strange events.

All help comes from the one stream of Mercy. If man imagines that it comes from other than Him it is because he sees himself. It is *ghurur* (غرور , deception), arrogance which leads to deception, self-conceit and being cut off from *tawhid* (توحيد,divine unity). The *kafir* (كفر , denier) who denies Allah's mercy is cut off from seeing the manifestation of *tawhid* in the perfection of the laws that govern existence.

From where does man's *rizq*, his provision, come? How is the recycling ecological continuum maintained? Because man is not in submission, his knowledge of creation is perverted. He only has limited knowledge which can only bring about momentary relief; this is arrogance. It cannot provide the fundamentally sound, inner understanding which can connect to the outer understanding. The knowledge of the One comes from within; it is the knowledge of the entire system.

أَفَمَن يَمْشِي مُكِبًّا عَلَىٰ وَجْهِهِ أَهْدَىٰ أَمَّن يَمْشِي سَوِيًّا عَلَىٰ صِرَاطٍ مُّسْتَقِيمٍ

22 **What! is he who goes prone upon his face better guided or he who walks upright upon a straight path?**

Mukibb (مكبّ , prostrated, dedicated) is from *kabba* (كب), to prostrate. Imam Rida, *'alayhi-s-salãm*, upon him be peace, when asked who were the people who had fallen flat on their faces, replied that they were those who did not obey the Prophet's injuction to follow 'Ali, *'alayhi-s-salãm*. Those who refused to follow "Ali, *'alayhi-s-salãm*, started to interpret for themselves. They assumed the belief that no *wasîy* (وصى , successor, deputy) had been nominated by the Prophet, *salla-llãhu 'alayhi wa ãlihi wa sallam*. How could such a wise being as the Prophet, *salla-llãhu 'alayhi wa ãlihi wa sallãm*, leave his people without appointing an appropriate man, who would bring about the full fruition of the gifts of Qur'ãn? No Muslim denies what the

Prophet, salla-llãhu 'alayhi wa ãlihi wa sallam, said about the *Ahl ul-Bayt* (family of the Prophet). Why do they not follow what is in the Qur'ãn and the *sunna* (سنة , sayings and doings of the Prophet)? Human beings wish to bring something of themselves into whatever they are given. When one is given a perfect recipe, there is the arrogance in one that desires to add some other ingredient. Unknowingly it may be poisonous to the liver.

There must be no interpretations; any interpretation will be a misinterpretation. The true slave is he who follows blindly and through his blindfold visualizes the light of his guidance. This is what gives *yaqin* (يقين), certainty. Otherwise, it is the fear of discovering that gives apparent strength.

The simple darkness of the blindfold makes some people adamant; that is not certainty. It may appear that they are very sure, but it is like the certainty of a despot compared to the certainty of the man of true îmãn and abandonment. The despot is sure of himself, but there is a point at which he cracks. The *mu'min* (believer) never cracks; if the afflictions increase he is increased in strength. When people turn away from him, he turns to Allah—that is from where real strength is derived. He who has abandoned into the true message and follows it diligently is on the clear path. He who has not is like one who has fallen upon his face.

There are degrees of îmãn. The ultimate *îmãn* is abandonment into Reality with knowledge-that is perfect harmony. As for those who have fallen upon themselves, they are Muslims who are misguided, *mu'minun* whose îmãn is incomplete or *kuffar* (كفار , plural of *kafir,* denier) who are in utter denial. These constitute fodder for the fire.

قُلْ هُوَ الَّذِىٓ أَنشَأَكُمْ وَجَعَلَ لَكُمُ السَّمْعَ وَالْأَبْصَارَ وَالْأَفْئِدَةَ ۖ قَلِيلًا مَّا تَشْكُرُونَ

23 **Say: He it is Who brought you into being and made for you the ears and the eyes and the hearts: little is it that you give thanks.**

Qul (قل), say, implies to witness, recognize and see the Creator. See how you have come about from the best of sources, the highest Source. See yourself, see how you hear and see. Reflect upon your heart, reflect upon your own situation. Then you will profess, confess and know that you have been created in the best form, in the highest form. It will bring gratitude, which will bring contentment, which in turn will bring greater sight and insight. *Qul huwa-llahu ahad,* "Say that Allah is One." (*al- Ikhlas*: 1). What is said often enough becomes what is meant and what is meant becomes what is said; then the created being sees only the One. By saying it he embraces *tawhid*.

"Little is it that you give thanks." Diving into the depths of the ãya yields greater comprehension of its inner meanings. By increasing one's contentment and gratitude, one is able to gain insight into one's creation and therefore into the Creator, hose attributes are contained in His creation.

قُلْ هُوَ الَّذِى ذَرَأَكُمْ فِى الْأَرْضِ وَإِلَيْهِ تُحْشَرُونَ

24 **Say: He it is Who scattered you on the earth and to Him you shall be gathered.**

وَيَقُولُونَ مَتَى هَذَا الْوَعْدُ إِن كُنتُمْ صَادِقِينَ

25 **And they say: When shall this threat be (executed) if you are truthful?**

قُلْ إِنَّمَا الْعِلْمُ عِندَ اللَّهِ وَإِنَّمَا أَنَا نَذِيرٌ مُّبِينٌ

26 **Say: The knowledge (thereof) is only with Allah and I am only a plain warner.**

فَلَمَّا رَأَوْهُ زُلْفَةً سِيئَتْ وُجُوهُ الَّذِينَ كَفَرُوا وَقِيلَ
هَذَا الَّذِي كُنتُم بِهِ تَدَّعُونَ

27 **But when they shall see it nigh, the faces of those who disbelieve shall be sorry, and it shall be said: This is that which you used to call for.**

Dharã (ذ را) means to scatter, disperse. Its related root of *dharra* (ذ ر) yields the Arabic words for atom (the smallest unit of anything) and offspring. For every action there is a reaction, for every scattering there is a gathering. Man has been scattered here in order to see the meaning of his existence, his reality, and his Source, to Which he will be gathered again.

Those who are not in the state of submission—who are not in an inner state of contentment, gratitude and therefor *tawhid,* and who do not see themselves as inseparable from Realit—see nothing other than discord; they are in *Kufr*. They ask when the promise of oneness will come to pass. If you are truthful, whne will the promise of *akhira* (آخرة , hereafter) be fulfilled. A man in doubt is constantly searching and asking for proof. The answer to the people of doubt emanates from the *îmãn* in one's heart—the heart has seen what is not and therefore dwells upon that which is.

The knowledge of the Unseen—the next world and the day of reckoning—is with Allah. Only a warning can be given to thsoe who deny. The *ãya* explains to those who ask about time that Allah is beyond time. Time exists so that man may take notice, pause, and reflect on what is behind it.

Warn them that to persist in questioning only increases doubt. It will sink them deeper into the quick and which they believe to be the solid ground upon which they rely. The system of *Kufr* perpetuates the illusion of its own firmness. In reality it has no foundation; it follows its *wahm* (وهم ,fancy, delusion), causing the seeker to seek in the wrong direction. His search leads him away from answers towards false hopes and despair. Man takes refuge in the bubble of *Kufr*. One strategic pric will burst it and cause both his own collapse and that of the system of *kufr*.

When the next life comes, those who formerly were in denial will wear an expression of contrition upon their faces. They will be in a dreadful state, having come face to face with that which they denied. They are told that this is what you were promised—you will be what you have earned. They have earned this state through their actions, which are backed by their intentions. In a tradition of the *Ahl ul-Bayt*, it is said that this *ãya* referes to some of the companions of the Prophet, *salla-llãhu 'alayhi wa ãlihi wa sallam*, who, upon seeing that 'Ali, *'alayhi-s-salãm*, was so close to the Prophet, were exceedingly jealous.

قُلْ اَرَءَيْتُمْ اِنْ اَهْلَكَنِيَ اللّٰهُ وَمَنْ مَّعِيَ اَوْ رَحِمَنَا فَمَنْ
يُّجِيْرُ الْكٰفِرِيْنَ مِنْ عَذَابٍ اَلِيْمٍ

28 **Say: Have you considered if Allah should destroy me and those with me — rather He will have mercy on us; yet who will protect the unbelievers from a painful punishment?**

Reality will cause everyone to perish. One must see that Allah's mercy and protection fall over everyone, whether *mu'min* or *kafir*. "Who will protect the unbelievers?" *Yujiru* (يجير) is from *ajara* (اجار), which means to protect or to aid someone. *Jãr* (جار) means neighbor; the word implies mercy and compassion. The *rahma* of Allah covers even he who denies at the moment of his denial. But whatever has a beginning has an end. A father's love for his son continues until he dies. The father has a contract with his son to be patient with him in every situation. But after the father dies, an uncle may take his place and treat the son roughly and impatiently. Everyone is given constant protection until he is woken up, whereupon there is regret for having left behind the remains of nothing but a miserable and misguided life. Allah has given everyone a respite, *ila ajalan musamma*, until an appointed time. The *Rahmãn* covers all beings with His beneficence and mercy. Understanding the rahma of Allah is attained by experiencing it whilst depending upon it.

قُلْ هُوَ الرَّحْمٰنُ اٰمَنَّا بِهٖ وَعَلَيْهِ تَوَكَّلْنَا ۚ فَسَتَعْلَمُوْنَ
مَنْ هُوَ فِيْ ضَلٰلٍ مُّبِيْنٍ

29 **Say: He is the Beneficent God, we believe in Him and on Him do we rely, so you shall come to know who it is that is in clear error.**

قُلْ أَرَءَيْتُمْ إِنْ أَصْبَحَ مَاؤُكُمْ غَوْرًا فَمَن يَأْتِيكُم بِمَآءٍ مَّعِينٍ

30 **Say: have you considered if your water should go down, who is it then that will bring you flowing water?**

"So you shall come to know who it is that is in clear error." A time comes to the Prophet, *salla-llãhu 'alayhi wa ãlihi wa sallam,* and to men of knowledge when there is nothing left to say. Having used *'aql* (عقل) and heart in every way possible to cause an awakening to occur, he can only say: You shall come to know.

Ghawr (غور) is a depression in the ground, from *ghãra* (غار), to sink in, become hollow, seep away. If your water is lost, there can be no sustenance. All beings depend upon water for their lives. The Qur'ãn says that all life is based upon water and that the throne—the *'arsh* (عرش), the foundation of creation—is afloat upon water. If there were no rock under the soil, only sand descending for miles, water would enter the earth and disappear. If all water is lost who will bring the flowing water? From where will it come? One's inner life is such that whenever there is arrogance, knowledge enters the questioning being like water and permeates down through an endlessly deep hole.

The state of being at a loss does not allow one to begin to reflect. Self-knowledge, the water that springs from the well of knowledge, does not stay; it passes on through and disappears into one's cave. The ghawr, the depression, is related in meaning to *nafaq* (نفق), underground tunnel. No matter how much knowledge you pour on the *mun-afiq* (منافق), the hypocrite, it will never take root because he always shakes it off, like a person who repeatedly escapes through tunnels. It is Allah's business to give water, to give sustenance, love, mercy; if there is reflection, then knowledge will remain.

The entire creation is the kingdom of the one and only King Whose attributes are known, Whose love is all-encompassing, Whose presence is beyond time, before time, in time and after time. One is able to initiate the growth of knowledge by momentarily stopping one's hypocrisy and lack of confidence and by admitting that one has nothing. If you have anything, it is by permission of He Who has created you. Allah has placed man on earth as a guardian, and that guardianship comes with responsibility, the responsibility of acknowledging his debt at all times to the merciful King of creation.

Author's Biography

Shaykh Fadhlalla Haeri was born in the Holy City of Karbala, Iraq, a descendant of five generations of well-known and revered spiritual leaders. Educated in Europe and America, Shaykh Fadhlalla obtained undergraduate and postgraduate degrees, majoring in science and engineering. As a businessman, he established several manufacturing and consulting firms in the Middle East, primarily in the oil industry. Shaykh Fadhlalla traveled extensively, especially in India, in pursuit of the spiritual teachings of the East, before his eventual re-discovery of the pure and original Islamic heritage of his birth.

In 1979, Shaykh Fadhlalla came to the United States to establish a spiritual foundation, the Zahra Trust, to enable serious students of Islam the opportunity of acquiring its basic teachings. The Zahra Trust currently publishes a wide variety of books through its affiliate, Zahra Publications, and has established several spiritual and medical centers in Asia, Europe and South America. The American Institute of Qur'ãnic Studies at Bayt-ud-Deen, the U.S. base of Zahra Trust, was inaugurated in December, 1981.

At present, Shaykh Fadhlalla is engaged in teaching, lecturing, and writing books and commentaries on the Holy Qur'ãn and related spiritual topics, with particular emphasis on inner meanings and '*irfan* (gnosis).

Forthcoming Books

By the same author :

Beginning's End

Beams of Illumination from the Divine Revelation

Heart of Qur'ãn and Perfect Mizan

The Journey of the Universe as Expounded in the Qur'ãn

The Light of Iman from the House of Imran

Living Islam

Man in Qur'ãn and the Meaning of Furqan

The Sufi Way to Self-Unfoldedment

The Journey of the Self